D1369914

THE
THREE-CAREER
COUPLE
Mastering the Art
of Juggling Work,
Home, and Family

CAR. DEV. GRANT

1295

8/16/95

18AT

THE THREE-CAREER COUPLE
Mastering the Art of Juggling Work, Home, and Family

Marcia Byalick and Linda Saslow

Peterson's
Princeton, New Jersey

Library of Congress Cataloging-in-Publication Data
Byalick, Marcia, 1947-
    The three-career couple / Marcia Byalick and Linda Saslow.
       p. cm.
    Includes index.
    ISBN 1-56079-239-6
    1. Dual-career families—United States. 2. Married people—Employment—United States. 3. Work and family—United States.
    I. Saslow, Linda, 1951- . II. Title.
HQ536.B93 1993
306.872—dc20   93-360

Cover and text design by Michael Freeland

Composition by Peterson's Guides

Printed in the United States of America

10 9 8 7 6 5 4 3 2 1

To our husbands and children, without whom this book would have been written in half the time.

ACKNOWLEDGMENTS

Written last and read first, acknowledgments are our opportunity to pay our debt to those kind souls who generously shared with us their wit, wisdom and experience.

To the professionals who offered their knowledge and gave us hours of suggestions, information and advice—

Ellen Galinsky, copresident of the Families and Work Institute, a nationally recognized nonprofit research and planning organization.

Michael Kimmel, professor of sociology at Stony Brook University in Stony Brook, New York, and one of the country's leading experts on gender and sexuality, national spokesman for the National Organization for Men Against Sexism, and editor of *Men's Lives.*

Dr. Arthur Mones, psychologist at the Family Therapy Training Program of the Long Island Institute of Psychoanalysis and faculty member of St. John's University in Jamaica, New York.

Dr. Raymond Havelick, director of the Institute for Psychosomatic Research in Roslyn, New York.

Dr. Jeffrey Lipner, a psychologist at the Nassau Center for Psychotherapy in Bellmore, New York.

Dr. Stuart Dolgin, a fellow of the American College of Gastroenterology.

Toni Liebman, former nursery school director, author and parent educator.

Joan Harris, president of a marketing agency and an expert in time management.

Gayle Rawlings, a counselor at Briarcliffe College in Hicksville, New York.

Adele Faber, author of *How to Talk So Kids Will Listen and Listen So Kids Will Talk* and other books on parenting and communication.

Sally Wendkos Olds, award-winning author of *The Working Parents' Survival Guide* and eight other books.

Mary Rose Paster, a psychologist specializing in family issues.

Judith Beckman, a certified financial planner, registered investment adviser, licensed stockbroker and president of Financial Solutions in Westbury, New York.

Shelley Freeman, director of personal financial planning at Shearson Lehman Brothers in New York City, a division of American Express.

Sally Ridgeway, a professor of sociology at Adelphi University in Garden City, New York.

Christopher Hayes, a director of the National Center for Women and Retirement Research at Long Island University, Southampton campus, Southampton, New York.

To those Three-Career Couples listed below who allowed us to use their names. And to those others who asked to remain anonymous but whose experiences were also helpful. All of these shared their experiences fine-tuning the new lifestyle that is our future:

Juliet and Alex Aurelio

Barbara and Bob Basta

Linda and Abner Bergman

Bonnie Byalick and Marshall Peller

Jean and Al Clark

Susan and Arthur Datz

Judy and Ken Davis

Carol and Bill Fisher

Diane and Richard Fromberg

Karen and Ken Gelb
Jane and Alan Gitlin
Carol and Fred Gruhle
Carole and Joe Hankin
Hope and Larry Kessler
Nanette and Steve Klein
Gail and Richard Kogan
Isabel and Howard Kogen
Renee and Alan Kronish
Leslie and Arthur Mones
Cathy and Charlie Northrop
Aileen and Elliot Paskoff
Enid and Richard Pinsker
Debbie and Burt Rapoport
Melanie and Glenn Rodriguez
Jacalyn and Ron Rudin
Jane and Barry Schweiger
Susan and Kent Seelig
Jill and Bob Sperling
Susan and Jan Starr
Joanne and Paul Stutz
Al and Lorry Trachtman
Carol and Bruce Ullman
Kathy and Larry Vedder
Elaine and Jay Viders
Karen and John Walczuk
Carol and Fred Weiss
Ilene and Mark Zelniker

And individually—

To our editor, Carol Hupping, who encouraged us, inspired us and made deadlines much less ominous.

To Susan Stegemann, for her patience, her research skills and her amazing deciphering ability.

To the staff of *The Women's Record,* for illustrating month after month that there is life after deadline.

To Michael Wexelbaum, whose expertise is only exceeded by his generosity.

To Fanny, whose experiences make clear that life's under no obligation to give us what we expect and who teaches daily that if we're smart, we'll be grateful it's not worse than it is.

And to our wonderful supportive families—

To Julie and Craig, who did without a kitchen table and a car pool driver and applauded their mom every step of the way.

To Jen and Carrie, who gave the best unsolicited, unearned, but badly needed hugs to a completely distracted mother.

And to Bob and Jerry, who ate leftovers without complaint, spent months of long, lonely Sundays while we approached our deadline and energized us throughout this project with the power of their love.

CONTENTS

INTRODUCTION

Both of us married at the tail end of the generation that thought that women should first have a family and then figure out how to fit work into their schedules. We write this book for the generation right behind us, for whom the opposite is now becoming the norm. Two decades ago we couldn't even open securities accounts without our husbands' signatures, and our husbands hadn't a clue as to how to turn on the washing machine. We began our three-career marriages at a time when home life was considered a barrier and a burden to accomplishment in the workplace.

Both of us met professionally years ago and recognized in each other a fellow tap dancer, another person preoccupied with the constant reshaping, restructuring and streamlining of the neverending lists that made up our lives. One of us, primarily a reporter immersed in facts and research, and the other, a columnist exploring issues of everyday concerns, immediately agreed we shared the need to be valued and appreciated for doing a pretty good job at making it all work.

We knew that only those trying to work their way through a similar daunting schedule could possibly understand what an accomplishment it really was. Far from striving for perfection, we just wanted to be reassured we were perpetrating no harm in the manner we were spending our limited time and energy. Since there was no standard on which to evaluate how well we were doing, we kept telling each other that if we couldn't give those we love the best of everything, that our very best would have to do.

We decided to collaborate on this project—part handbook, part resource, part inspiration—because it was the kind of book we wished we could have read early on. We are keenly aware that the experiences we give our children will determine the family our grandchildren will grow up in. Although women are no longer viewed as dependents and men are no longer just passive bystanders at home and their union is no longer based on an exchange of services, many marriages lapse into behaviors as if these statements were still true. Life constantly challenges us with the fact that everything we do can be done better. By clarifying some issues, problem solving some solutions and inspiring some confidence, we hope to help you through the situations where all your careful coordination and hard work don't seem enough to get the job done. For the times you feel you're on a baseball team with only eight players in the field. For when your prime childbearing years collide painfully with the most demanding of your career. For when you'd give all the money in your wallet for one quiet hour of introspection and reflection.

During the 80s, the term "dual-career couple" became a part of most vocabularies as this growing population received greater media attention and became a source of increasing interest among psychologists, marriage counselors, financial planners and experts in time and stress management. With the 90s came the acknowledgment that we were not a fleeting breed but one that is here to stay.

We are the role models for the next generation, who are now watching us as we try our hardest to master the fine art of juggling our many responsibilities. No longer can we afford to minimize the importance of our Third Career—our home and our family. To ensure that healthy families flourish in homes where time is life's most valuable commodity, the family unit must be headed by a strong—and equitable—partnership. Negotiating our way through the uncharted waters of balancing power, ego and career advancement with parenting, responsibility and love, we are doing our best to integrate and survive three careers. We are a generation of Three-Career Couples.

As Three-Career Couples we share many concerns and questions. Is there any solution for our chronic "Hurried and Worried Syndrome"? How can we find more time for each other? Is there a better way to cope with stress, manage time, make career decisions as a team? We can't promise easy answers or magic solutions. Instead, we've tried to offer a unique blend of suggestions, strategies and practical advice from professional experts in fields including psychology, finance, communication, stress and time management; of information—statistics, surveys and studies—that you may fine surprising, reassuring, or at the least, interesting; and of personal stories (both successes and failures!) from real people who graciously shared with us their experiences facing the daily demands, dilemmas and decisions of Three-Career Couples.

We found practical advice in the words of these couples learning to see everyday problems as opportunities for growth and mastery. By interviewing 80 Three-Career Couples, first through a 50-question short-answer survey, and then in person, we found the truth in the statement "Every person you meet knows something you don't." This sampling all shared these basic truisms. That:

1) Nothing is as important as it seems at the moment.

2) You can keep going long after you thought you could.

3) It's tough not neglecting the uniqueness of today because we're so preoccupied with tomorrow.

4) No solution will work if it doesn't respect the dignity of both husband and wife.

Not one couple bragged about how well they were handling having it all. Not one could point to any family they envied for doing it "the right way." And each participant was generous with his or her time and was eager to contribute, hoping to pick up a tip or two along the way.

Sometimes the statements and names are verbatim; sometimes they're disguised or a compilation of several views. We found the words of our couples to be more reliable than many of the statistics we came across. Time and again we found numbers and percentages varying widely. We included those in the book that were corroborated by more than one source or came from research we regarded as unbiased and honest.

We're a generation on the go, in the know, forced to keep moving fast just to maintain our place. Vince Lombardi once said, "Winning isn't everything, but wanting to win is." Well, perfectly executing every task on your list for the day isn't everything, but creatively overcoming obstacles, learning through discipline and teamwork to find solutions and taking advantage of the opportunity to shape a brave new world (with a minimum of heartburn and upset stomachs) truly is. Life might have been a lot simpler years ago, but it was never richer. Hang tough. It's worth it.

NOW THAT WE HAVE IT ALL, WOULD YOU LIKE SOME?
Challenges and Benefits of the Three-Career Couple

Why not go out on a limb? Isn't that where the fruit is?
Frank Scully, *Forbes*

Boy oh boy, aren't *we* the coolest generation of all time. As Three-Career Couples, we sloughed off the conditioning that designated our behaviors and abilities genetically fixed. We've forsaken the safe and familiar for lives made up of a myriad of new customized arrangements. Every problem we solve, every dragon we slay, is ours alone.

"I have a uterus and a brain and they both work," said Congresswoman Patricia Schroeder, speaking for herself and millions of other women. Those women who make up 45 percent of our labor force[1] know there's no turning back. And their husbands, beginning their odyssey of redefinition a bit later than their wives, are slowly becoming more flexible, more open and less bound to the restraints of being the stereotypical "head of the household."

Even though their actions may sometimes suggest otherwise, 81 percent of men in a 1991 survey agreed with the statement "men have as much responsibility for taking care of household chores as women do."[2] And 45 percent of the 500 working men polled by Robert Half International, an international recruiting firm in the finance field, said they might turn down a promotion if it meant spending less time with their families.[3] No more do stereotypes set limits on what we can accomplish, what we can expect and what we think we are worth. Negotiating our way without the road map of our parents' experience, both men and women are realizing the differences between us are not as great as those between rich and poor or old and young. And the friendship between us is becoming a commodity more valued than gold.

Even corporations, not usually known for their humanistic virtues, are gradually coming to understand the importance of family and personal relations in their workers' lives. When studies show that 50 percent of those polled would sacrifice a day's pay for an extra day off a week,[4] when eight out of ten said in a 1990 *Los Angeles Times* survey of 1,000 households that they rank the most important things in their lives to be family, marriage and love—with financial security, work and career following[5]—then companies like Corning and Aetna, IBM and Johnson and Johnson begin to be more sensitive to the fact that satisfying each employee's personal agenda will ultimately lead to greater productivity.

Some important changes have taken place in the most forward-thinking corporations—and they're coming along, albeit more slowly, in other workplaces, says Ms. Galinsky, copresident of the Families and Work Institute (a nationally recognized nonprofit research and planning organization in New York). In the coming decade, work will be redefined. "As the anytime, anyplace office becomes more commonplace (faxes and computers in the home, phones in cars), and as the United States moves toward an information-based economy, boundaries between work and family will become even more diffuse. Standards for measuring performance are expected to hinge less on presence (the number of hours one works equals commitment and productivity) and more on results," she explains.[6]

Institutions Are Changing but Just not Fast Enough

Lest we give you the impression that *all* corporations are better accommodating two-income families than ever before, we highlight the findings of the 1992 Work and Family Report by Ellen Galinsky, copresident of the Families and Work Institute, which presents a mixed outlook. Ms. Galinsky says, "It is now more widely understood that work-family problems are a result of families changing faster than institutions—than the workplace with its last-minute meetings or mandatory overtime, than the schools that provide little warning of events that parents are expected to attend, than doctors and dentists who don't have evening hours or than banks that close at three o'clock."

According to Ms. Galinsky, some work-family assistance exists in all large companies, but most companies have a limited or piecemeal approach. Based on several studies by the Families and Work Institute, which classified companies into distinct stages of development, it was found that among large companies:

- 33% are in Pre-Stage I, with few policies and management resistance or bare awareness of the issues.

- 46% are in Stage I, with several policies but not a packaged response; work-family is seen mainly as a women's issue with a focus on child care.

- 19% are in Stage II, with an integrated approach to meeting the work-family needs of employees.

- 2% are in Stage III, with a focus that has moved beyond programs toward changing the company culture to be more family and community friendly.[7]

Even among companies with programs in place, few offer time and leave flexibility. Studies of employee populations conducted by the Families and Work Institute reveal that the kind of assistance employed parents most desire is greater time flexibility—to be able to take leaves to be with a new baby or sick child, to be able to be late without censure if there is a child care problem or their child has trouble separating in the morning, to be able to attend a school play or a teacher's conference or to be able to take an elderly parent to the doctor. While most large companies do have time-off policies, only 45 percent are written into company policy, and only one fourth are available companywide.[8]

Although most of corporate America is moving slower than we'd like it to when it comes to instituting new programs, subtle changes in attitude portend a tolerance for a more humanistic view in the future. The goals of self-fulfillment and career development haven't been abandoned, but the days of bragging about going to the office on weekends and bringing work on vacation are numbered. It's seldom true anymore that if you leave the office early once in a while to watch your son pitch in a Little League game or take time off for a long weekend to celebrate an anniversary, you're considered a less than desirable employee.

MEN: ARE YOU READY FOR A 50-50 PARTNERSHIP?

The United States Department of Labor didn't even keep statistics before 1950 on how many women with children under one year old worked. Today it's 50 percent.[9] According to this bureau, in 1990 employed women earned about 30 percent of the total family income.[10] Ninety-four percent of the women work because they need the money.[11] By sharing the breadwinning burden some hoped their spouses would work less and contribute more at home.

9-5, the National Association of Working Women, tells us there are 56 million women in the work force shouldering by choice or by default more than their fair share of the familial responsibilities.[12] The financial realities behind these rising numbers have led us to prepare our daughters as we prepare our sons for a life where in the future the only pedestals they'll see will be those placed under statues.

Men are becoming increasingly more comfortable with the notion of a working wife. In fact, it's a new badge of courage to be the spouse of a financially contributing, perhaps even prestigious, working woman. However, they haven't given up entirely on the tidy house and whiter whites of their fantasies. They might be ready to forfeit the role of conquering hero, but their upbringing and socialization have not prepared them for anything approaching a 50-50 working partnership at home. As their roles have expanded over the last two decades, women have been forced to make enormous changes. Now it is their husbands' turn to make comparable adjustments.

One of the reasons for this time lag between men's and women's changes is that men are afraid, says T. Berry Brazelton, one of America's best-known pediatricians and educators. In his book *Working and Caring* he writes, "When men see that women are capable of managing two roles successfully it uncovers an unconscious fear—that women really are the dominant sex."[13]

Many men distance themselves from home and family because they fear their own failures as nurturers, says Michael Kimmel, Ph.D., Professor of Sociology at Stony Brook University and one of the country's leading experts on gender and sexuality. Dr. Kimmel, well known as the national spokesman for the National Organization for Men Against Sexism and editor of *Men's Lives,* a best-selling textbook, believes that there is nothing magical, mystical or genetically transmitted when it comes to nurturing. There are no inborn traits that make women better equipped to push a stroller, drive a car pool or read a bedtime story. Nurturing is based on a set of skills that are learned; the more you do them the better you get.

Men also resist change because they perceive they stand nothing to gain and much to lose. They grew up with images of what real men are like; taking an active role in what goes on at home means becoming a wimp. After all, John Wayne never did a dish, Sylvester Stallone never changed a diaper.

But the rules of the game are changing and now it's the men's challenge to learn to play by them. Where is it written that respecting your partner as an equal makes you weak? It does, in fact, make you stronger. "We men have a choice," says Dr. Kimmel. "We can either be dragged kicking and screaming into it, or we can say, 'What's in it for us?'"

THE THREE-CAREER COUPLE

The "dual-career couple" is a familiar expression—two partners pursuing their own separate careers. The "three-career couple" may not be so familiar to us as a term, but it's not new anymore as a concept. The Third Career—their "job" together—acknowledges the importance of the home and family life they share.

Today's true Three-Career Couple recognizes that both partners can and should be productive and ambitious in their careers outside the home and productive and nurturing in the

Third Career they share in the home. This modern couple is willing to sacrifice some of its time alone, some of its leisure, some of its commitment to work for a shot at the new true American Dream: A balanced work and home life with an equitable distribution of tasks, resulting in honest, healthy, successful family relationships.

The Three-Career Couple has its work cut out for it. Women have to stop behaving like nags and martyrs; men have to start giving them less reason to feel that way. Women have to be clearer about what they need; men have to see the benefits they will reap if they cooperate more fully.

As the definition of the Three-Career Couple continues to be refined, so, too, will the concept of masculinity. The image of a man who orders his priorities as work, sports, fast cars and family, who's never cooked a meal or pushed a vacuum, is quietly being replaced by a man who can be relied upon, who is there when he's needed.

Men who welcome these changes, who are ready to catch up with their partners, are those who stand to gain the most in their personal lives. "We men will live better lives if we live with women who are our equals," explains Dr. Kimmel. We will have:

- better relationships with our wives
- better relationships with our children
- better friendships with other men

"This is not a big loss," says Dr. Kimmel. "On the contrary, we're the winners!".

When historians look back a hundred years from now, the 80s will be remembered as the decade Mom went back to work, and the 90s will be known as the decade we started to get it right. Change is tough, especially when our behavior has been conditioned by stereotypes that don't work anymore; by expectations that are no longer realistic. Our task is to keep alive the parts of the relationship we cherish and to integrate those with the practical realities of today's world.

"I fell in love with Jackie on our first date—when she made dinner and set the table with cloth napkins," says Ron, a 38-year-old internist. "I knew she was a successful matrimonial lawyer with a great mind and a terrific sense of humor, but it was the cloth napkins, evidence of a woman who's a nester, that really got me. When I opened the refrigerator and saw it was fuller than my grandmother's, complete even to horseradish, three kinds of mustard, fresh garlic and salsa, I knew I was going to marry her. I proposed three weeks later, giving her an ID bracelet inscribed, 'Feathers between us forever.'"

It's difficult, however, to preserve the domestic heritage of our mothers while tap dancing through the tag team arrangements necessary to make modern family life run smoothly. In the 80s, TV shows like *LA Law* portrayed the foremost realm of intimacy and fulfillment—for both men and women—to be the workplace. Children were nonexistent and relationships at home took a distinctly secondary role. Now, after mastering the importance of "being your own person," the ground has shifted and we're being asked to "be your own couple."

"The best thing about being part of a Three-Career Couple is that we never run out of things to talk about," says Andrea, 35, a nutritionist married to John, also 35 and a chiropractor. "There are new stories every day from our jobs. Life never gets stale."

"I couldn't imagine life without working," admits Vicki, 32, a buyer for a department store, wife and mother of a two-year-old daughter. "It's that daily charge of my batteries that energizes me, makes me feel productive and creative, and I'm convinced makes me a better wife and mother to Ali."

And from Shelley, 36, a bookkeeper and mother of three children under 12: "Let's face it; it would be impossible to make ends meet today if either Gary or I were not working. Before I started working two years ago, every time one of the kids asked for a new pair of sneakers, I cringed. Now with two salaries we can afford to pay our bills, go out for dinner without feeling guilty and take a family vacation for a week every summer. We're in a comfort zone that allows us to get by without being in a constant state of anxiety."

Despite the challenges of integrating work and home, the testimonies from Three-Career Couples we interviewed project a positive feeling, focusing on the practical and psychological rewards—both to the marriage and to the family. Our sample, an admittedly unscientific survey of 80 two-income couples who volunteered to share their experiences, cut across economic, geographic and political lines. What they had in common was a belief that they were on the road to getting it right, that they were still improvising daily and that the only solutions that work are those arrived at by working closely as a team.

According to Dr. Arthur Mones, a psychologist at the Family Therapy Training Program of the Long Island Institute of Psychoanalysis, the benefits that the Three-Career Couple bring to their marriage include:

- Feelings of individual accomplishment and self-fulfillment. Partners who feel better about themselves can offer more to each other.

- Exposure to new ideas and attitudes, which leads to added knowledge, skills and competence.

- Increased closeness between partners as intellectual companions.

- A wider range of social, business and professional relationships and friendships.

- Increased income, which yields more financial benefits—or at least can lessen anxiety about money and provide a safety blanket in these shaky economic times.

AND BABY MAKES CHAOS

Even those couples who work beautifully as a team will admit that when you add children to the equation, home life and careers can go careening into orbit. Again, there are no hard-and-fast rules. We hand kids off to a variety of nannies, sitters, schools, day care centers, neighbors and relatives and pray for the best. Our children are not being raised as we were (not that that was perfection, by any means), and we have to keep ourselves from worrying that we have absolutely no idea how it will all turn out. The home-baked cookies, hand-ironed shirts and canasta games that greeted youngsters at 3 p.m. have been replaced by a patchwork of informal home arrangements and more structured day care options. It is often difficult for working partners to realize the rewards of a three-career family—buried as they are beneath layers of stress, exhaustion, worry and guilt.

"Before Nicki was born, it was no big deal managing two careers," says Joanne, 39, a social worker and mother of a four-year-old daughter. "But with a child, things are different. The guilt of leaving Nicki and going to work is sometimes unbearable. When I'm away from her, she's always on my mind. I'm so pulled that I never feel like I'm doing a good job—not at work, not at home."

Partners may disagree on many issues, but most concur that working two jobs and raising children is not easy. Working mothers worry that they are not as involved in their children's activities as they'd like and that not having enough time together will cause their children to suffer.

In a 1991 report to the President and Congress by the U.S. Merit Systems Protection Board titled Balancing Work Responsibilities and Family Needs, women employed full- or part-time were asked: "How often do you feel torn between the demands of your job and the desire to spend more time with your family?" Seventy-five percent of them responded sometimes or very often.[14]

Early theories stressed only the negative effects on children caused by their mothers working out of the home. Providing some comfort to Three-Career Couples are recent studies that show that in an average week mothers employed full-time are found to spend only about five hours less with schoolage children than are nonemployed mothers.[15] (A variety of child care options pick up the slack.) And, reassuringly, research has revealed that only 36 percent of adults whose mothers worked when they were children said that it would've been better for them if their mothers had not worked outside the home.[16]

"I really think that Jamie is much better off with Jackie as a working mother," says Ron. "If all that energy, that passion, that devotion that Jackie puts into her career were showered totally on Jamie, I think she'd drown."

Even though working parents and partners continue to worry as routinely as they breathe, most of the couples you'll meet throughout this book agree there are significant benefits to having children *and* careers. In addition to the pluses pointed out by Dr. Mones earlier, the couples we spoke to find there is:

- More flexible division of labor between parents. Children are less likely to grow up with sexist attitudes and are more likely to view both men and women as breadwinners and both men and women as nurturers.

- A sharing of household responsibilities with their children. Parents agree that this often instills children with a sense of independence and helps them to become more self-confident and resourceful.

- More intimate contact between children and their fathers. Husbands of working women are more likely to be involved in child care than husbands of wives who don't work. This contributes to more intimate contact and a closer relationship between children and their fathers.

- More contact for children with other children and adults through various child care options. Children of working parents are likely to have greater exposure to other children and adults, benefiting their intellectual and emotional development.

- Increased child contact with the work world. This is likely to introduce children to new ideas and attitudes.

- Greater efficiency in the home. Their households tend to be more structured and tightly organized, teaching children important skills at the earliest opportunity.

It is said that children know their parents better than parents know their children because those in power are studied very carefully by those they control. What our children will tell their psychoanalysts twenty years from now is anyone's guess!

In a 1990 *Parents* poll, 40 percent of those surveyed said the impact of the changes brought about when both spouses work can be negative to family life.[17] We've heard the prophets of doom and gloom blame everything from teen suicide to the hole in the ozone layer on the disintegrating family values they see as stemming from Mom's spending her time earning money to buy new socks rather than darning the old ones. We can't argue that the days before the concept of latchkey children and instant mashed potatoes seem simpler—but they're gone. And the fact that 73 percent of the men and 71 percent of the women say they would keep working, even if they suddenly became wealthy, reinforces the notion that these trends are irreversible.[18]

TIME IS THE BIGGEST CULPRIT

Of the many challenges facing the Three-Career Couple, the one on the top of most lists is lack of time: lack of time for each other, ourselves, our children, homes, daily responsibilities and errands.

Are You in Control of Your Life?

Every deadline is met and the kitchen floor is clean. You're in control, doing an excellent job coping with the challenges of the Three-Career Couple—or are you? The 18-question quiz that follows will tell you where you stand. Score one point for each "yes" response.

1) Are you the only one on your block who doesn't know the zip code for Beverly Hills?

2) Do you work later than 5:30 p.m. more than once a week?

3) Have all your houseplants died?

4) Are you annoyed when someone you recently met doesn't ask you what you do for a living?

5) Do you ever dream of coming down with a titch of pneumonia—where bed rest is mandatory for two or three days?

6) Does your stomach tighten, neck grow stiff or head start to pound when you realize that it's time to:

a) bring the car in for a tune-up?

b) service the vacuum (or any appliance that has to be brought to a repair shop)?

c) renew your license?

d) take your dog to the vet?

7) Do you think back longingly to a past when half hour baths, long gossipy phone calls and reading for pleasure were a taken-for-granted part of everyday life?

8) Have you visited the supermarket after 9:00 p.m. more than once this month?

9) Do you have more than three people in your life that you feel bad about "owing" a phone call?

10) Does every fastfood establishment within five miles of your home know you by name?

11) When you pass dishes in the sink or towels on the floor or an unmade bed on your way out the door in the morning, do you feel less accomplished and not as worthwhile?

12) Are the holidays more stressful (because of the preparation they entail) than pleasurable?

13) Have you put off making a doctor or a dentist appointment for yourself because this just isn't a good time?

14) Is the thought of having a dinner party or entertaining a group of friends overwhelming?

15) Do you bring work home with you more than twice a month?

16) If faced with the choice of fewer working hours or more money, would you go for the bucks?

17) Do you wind up reading the magazines you subscribe to weeks (or months) after they arrive?

18) Have you ever caught yourself thinking about work during sex?

Results:

15 or more points: If all those in control of their lives were asked to stand, we'd make you sit down.

10 to 14 points: It could be worse—you could have known it was going to be like this years ago.

5 to 9 points: You're getting there, but you still have a way to go.

4 or fewer: Good work. Now reward yourself with a vacation that's longer than one week—and don't tell anyone at work where you're going!

———————————

"There aren't enough hours in a day," complains Paul, a computer analyst in his early forties and father of four-year-old Nicki. "I don't have time to do even the simplest things. I spent my one-week summer vacation catching up on long overdue silly errands that I never have time to do while I'm working. I needed a new pair of sneakers; then I lost my sunglasses and my gym bag ripped. The two hours that I spent one morning by myself in a local mall taking care of all those little things were satisfying in a way only someone in my position could ever understand."

"The best gift I could ever ask for would be for more time," says Ellen, 33, an architect and mother of two preschool daughters. "My favorite daydream is that I'm walking along the beach, sort of gliding in slow motion like I don't have a care in the world. As I'm walking, I pull off my watch and casually toss it into the ocean. Then I keep gliding along, with a big grin on my face."

Time, indeed, is the biggest culprit. But following close behind are complaints of:

- Exhaustion: "We're always tired. By the time we get home at night our best intentions—of cooking a great dinner together, taking a walk into town for frozen yogurt or playing a game of Monopoly with the kids—often get waylaid because we're so cranky or postponed for another day because we're just too pooped!"

- Guilt: "Whatever I'm doing, it isn't enough."

- Unrealistic expectations: "We're both efficient, competent adults; why should it be so difficult to find more time for ourselves and for each other, keep the house clean and the kids happy without always feeling like we're on the verge of a nervous breakdown? "

- Unrelenting stress: "Before I went back to work, I'd suffer with PMS once a month for a few days," says Susan, a 37-

year-old nursery school teacher and mother of three. "You know, that terrible stressed-out, about-to-explode feeling—not sure at any given moment whether to scream or to bawl. Now, at times that have nothing to do with my hormones, I still have that feeling. I love my job, but I wish I could just split myself in half. From Monday to Friday I'm a bundle of nerves—worrying about the kids while I'm at work, agonizing over not having enough time to fit everything into a day. I'm never relaxed—what if one of the kids needs me when I'm not home? What am I going to make for dinner? How will I have time to pick up the laundry detergent and the toothpaste? It's neverending. I'm always tired, always tense, often on the verge of tears."

KEEPING ALL THE BALLS IN THE AIR

You can have it all, just not all at once. When the pressure mounts and the tension builds and affection dwindles and romance becomes a memory, remember that juggling three balls in the air (your career, your family/yourself) is a skill that every person in the world is initially clumsy learning and one that inevitably improves with practice. Balance is the key word here and maintaining it is a lot tougher than we ever thought it would be.

We know that if there's a hurricane approaching we need to get flashlights, save water and tape the windows. If we feel tremors in the ground, we race to a doorway. For an impending snowfall, we stock up on shovels, batteries and rock salt. But the crises that befall Three-Career Couples can happen time and time again, and we're particularly slow at incorporating survival techniques to help us get through them.

"We are a can-do society," says Dr. Raymond Havelick, director of the Institute for Psychosomatic Research in Roslyn, New York. "We make a commitment, then figure out later whether it's possible, feasible or even desirable. This is typical of almost everything we do in our culture. We don't believe in planning. We are a crisis-oriented civilization. We react after the crisis and typically the reaction to make things better is patchwork and rarely deals with the underlying forces."

How much of "it all" do we need each day to make us happy? How much money, how many kisses, how polished the banisters, how low a cholesterol level—must we have to feel good about our lives? We've been battered over the head for years with the importance of compromise as the number-one behavior to facilitate successful relationships, but when the rules of the 90s family are so flexible as to be almost nonexistent and exactly what is required and expected of each partner is so idiosyncratic, we have to sort out the details before working on our communication skills.

All successful people have a passion to succeed that grounds them. They are clear about what they want, they don't dwell on limitations, and, very importantly, they have the courage to take risks. In a three-career marriage, the focus must not be on who works when but on how the family works out its way of caring in the nature of its day-to-day experiences. With cultural values shifting toward a greater concern for family well-being, the issue is not how many hours they work but how comfortably they shift the third-career work load from one partner to the other.

As you read this book, it's important you don't blame yourself for experiencing difficulty juggling the complicated elements of work responsibilities and the challenges of a satisfying home life. Because it's stressful and exhausting this moment doesn't mean it will always be so.

No one should expect to travel the road to attaining this mastery alone. When partners work as a team, effective balancing becomes a less overwhelming feat. Teamwork should begin with a cooperative evaluation of expectations, according to Toni Liebman, a New York early childhood specialist who conducts professional workshops for parents and educators in the workplace and at schools.

Realistic expectations for yourself, your spouse, your children, your home and your job are vital in order to create a healthy balance.

In your life you are a person, a partner, a worker, and maybe a parent. At different times, as needs change, more energy must go into the different people you are, often requiring a lowering of expectations in some of the other categories.

If you think you can do it all, be it all, have it all, snap out of it—that much success must be fatal because we've never met a person that lucky who's survived. Unrealistic expectations are a guarantee to failure.

As partners regularly reevaluate their expectations, they can choose which areas need more of their time and energy and work together to find ways to shortcut the others. If children are willing to participate in household chores, parents must ignore lumpy beds and dinner tables set backwards. If it's a particularly demanding day at work and you wind up substituting a pizza or deli sandwiches for a home-cooked dinner, who's going to remember it a week later? As the kids say, "Chill."

Sally and Fred, law partners both in their late thirties, love to entertain, but between their long hours and family demands, they couldn't get it together to host dinner parties the way they used to when they were first married. Their solution: a monthly "gourmet dinner club" with a group of close friends; the hosts choose the theme for the evening, and each guest brings a favorite dish.

For both Carole and Joe, in their early fifties, housework has never been a priority and their expectations of a perfect house were easily compromised. Clipped to the refrigerator with a smiley face magnet is a three-by-five card reminding anybody who passes, "A perfect house is the sign of a wasted life." "Messiness has never bothered either of us," says Carole, a public school superintendent. "We have no problem closing bedroom doors and forgetting what's inside. Joe and I are both okay with this system, as long as the mess doesn't creep into the entrance foyer where it would hit you immediately."

SUMMING IT UP

What we all need is the competent wife of yesteryear to come along in her housecoat and uncomplicate our lives. Unfortunately, she appears as often today as Tinkerbell and the Tooth Fairy. The Three-Career Couple, two-income earners who have a Third Career at home, must learn to incorporate *her* work load into *their* world.

Becoming more comfortable as partners in your work both within and outside of the home will lead you, as a "new" Three-Career Couple to:

■ Have more realistic expectations—of yourselves, of each other and of your three careers. You may still strive to "have it all," but you will realize that it can't "all" necessarily be at the same time. You've gone this long without being sublimely happy, what's a few more decades before you get it right?

■ Share concerns, frustrations, pleasures: what you need from each other and for yourselves; negotiate and compromise to come up with a team plan that will work for both partners. Like Madonna says, "You can't get what you want if you don't ask for it." It's so basic. It should be so easy—but it's not.

■ Look for new and creative ways to find romantic getaways, use family time optimally and treat yourself to a bit of self-indulgence once in a while.

HELP ME FIND IT BEFORE I LOSE IT!
Holding On to One's Sanity, Coping with Stress, Eliminating Guilt

Americans are forever brooding over advantages they do not possess.
It is strange to see with what feverish ardor they pursue their own
welfare, and to watch the vague dread that constantly torments them
lest they should not have chosen the shortest path
which may lead to it.

Alex de Toqueville, 1830

Mothers used to say when they entered the netherworld of overload, when they were no longer able to deal effectively with problems large and small, at work or at home, that they were "nervous." Fathers, inhabiting the same uncomfortable state, said they were "tense." Today, when life is teetering out of control, when we're on a plane and begin imagining it wouldn't be so bad to go down rather than have to complete the agenda we've mapped out for the next few days, we nonsexistly acknowledge that we're "stressed."

Actually, although we're not always stressed, there are days when we pass the point where stress adds flavor, challenge and opportunity to life. That's when we arrive at the road's end, where prolonged stress leaves us feeling "nibbled to death by ducks." Welcome to distress, where career and family commitments collide. Chances are, you're already immune to well-meaning jargon saying how you must "take care of yourself," how you should relax, how you should stop letting precious hours slip by, how you should just make time to read a good book. And the last thing you need in your life is another list of "shoulds."

"I hear all the time about priorities," says Susan, a teacher and mother of two who's going for her master's degree. "What should I not do? Drive the kids to school? Finish my lesson plans? Fold the laundry? Pick up Melanie's medicine at the drugstore? People say, Simplify your life. Do only what's essential. But that's all I do—and it's killing me."

"Sometimes," says Arthur, her husband and a financial planner, "I wake up so tense I want to snarl at the world. I feel like I'm surrounded by idiots . . . and the day hasn't even started. Then I try to focus on something relaxing—rocking on a hammock, for example, anything to pull me out of this revved-up, wild-eyed state. The joke is, I aggravate myself even more when I remember the last time I *did* have the opportunity to lie down on a hammock—I was nudgy in five minutes and got up feeling unaccomplished and nonproductive."

Arthur is not alone in finding that being at ease is difficult. The constant quest to cram one more thing into an already jam-packed day is taking its toll. Whole industries cater to alleviating the aches and pains our too-full days inflict on our bodies. Been to the drugstore to buy aspirin lately? For a generation sophisticated enough to rattle off the percentage of fat in our bodies, monitor our cars' gas emissions and buy bottled water, why do we need 17 different kinds of pain relievers? Who among us admits to stashing these bottles in kitchen cabinets, bedroom nighttables, purses, office drawers and cars? And what is it about the way we're conducting our lives that makes us feel we need to protect ourselves from the certain onslaught of distress? How many of the following ways has your body expressed its displeasure with the way you're living your life this week?

1) increased heart rate
2) sweating
3) stiff neck
4) lower back pain
5) knot in your stomach
6) skin breakout
7) sour stomach/digestive problems
8) headaches

If you only mention your energy and sex drive in the past tense, along with fond memories of your sense of humor or a good night's sleep, chances are you're overextended. If you're walking a seven-day-a-week treadmill where you're sweating a lot but winding up in the same place, it's safe to say you're living out of balance. And if planning to have some fun seems like it's not worth the effort, it's time to decrease the number of your activities and recalibrate the inner rhythm that has given your life too fast a pace.

It's simplistic to believe that if your salary were bigger or the kids were older or your spouse were more understanding or you traded in your house for a low-maintenance condo, your anxiety and worry would disappear. We are a hurried society, brimming with ambition. It's a lethal combination of key factors that tip average stress into overload, exposing us at our most unlovable. Just when we need our spouses the most, it's the hardest to tell them. We snap and deny that we're irritable. We blame our partners for not protecting us from a world that needs us too much. We grow disgusted with ourselves and withdraw from any possibility of cuddles. And we become inflexible, unwilling to even listen to alternative scheduling ideas.

Stress usually comes from one of two places—work or home. If it's work related, it's likely you feel that

1) you're stuck in a job you don't like;

2) there are less than desirable working conditions on the job;

3) you have too much responsibility and therefore too much pressure;

4) you have too much work and not enough time to accomplish it;

5) you don't have enough responsibility—leaving you with feelings of self-doubt, inadequacy, boredom and insecurity about your future in the job;

6) there are problems in relationships with others at work; and/or

7) a negative change in some facet of the job: assignments, staff, organization, procedures.

If your stress is home related, it's likely you feel that

1) there's tension in your marriage stemming from incompatible expectations or a lack of communication;

2) you have overwhelming responsibilities with your children;

3) you have financial burdens;

4) you have pressure from aging parents, in-laws or other relatives;

5) there are social pressures from friends or community obligations; and/or

6) overwhelming household responsibilities.

The good news is that there are, of course, ways to straighten yourself out. Accepting the responsibility for extricating yourself from potentially lethal-to-your-mental-health situations is the first step. Just as you can make yourself sick trying to fulfill megacommitments, you can make yourself well again by assigning stress alleviation the highest priority.

Reducing stress is a process that rests on several key elements:

1) learning to recognize symptoms of stress and what activates them

2) making some necessary changes in your lifestyle

3) incorporating "stress busters" into your daily schedule

4) coming up with effective ways to really relax

5) being kind to your body

6) finding reasons to laugh (Laughter is one way for us to release stress and feel good all over. A surge in the number of comedy clubs and a comedy channel now on cable TV attest to a society responding to our needs.)

WHAT PUSHES YOUR STRESS BUTTONS?

A situation that causes one person to stress out may be energizing to another. Oral presentations, children's birthday parties, high school reunions, even wallpapering the bedroom are examples of either opportunities or dreaded events, depending on your perspective. Recognizing what pushes your buttons can help you learn how to either cope with or avoid stressful situations.

Easing stress begins with understanding it. Just like the mind protects us by blocking from our conscious memory exactly

what pain feels like (who would ever have a second child?), so
it sometimes refuses to keep handy the cues to what unnerves
us. Let yourself dwell for a moment or two on each of the
points here. Take comfort from the fact that it's truly tough trying to maintain equilibrium in what is often a challenging and
demanding life.

1) Don't get tense about being tense; don't expect too much
   from yourself. Remind yourself of what you do well and
   be forgiving of what you don't.

2) Learn to tell the difference between what you can change
   and what you can't.

3) Learn to know yourself—what exactly is it about that
   colleague that makes your back teeth clamp down? About
   the supermarket that gives you a headache?

4) Keep a sense of perspective—when things start to build,
   ask yourself if the situation is worth what it's costing.

5) Live in the present. Don't dwell on past mistakes with "if
   only" or dream about "some day" in the future. Concentrate on *today*. Today's stress will pass.[1]

6) Realize that you are not alone. Analyze your support networks and decide which can be counted on and for what.

STRESS IS EXHAUSTING!

Everyday happenings like deadlines, unpaid bills and not
enough time to read the newspaper can become stomachache
producers. According to Dr. Jeffrey Lipner, a psychologist at
the Nassau Center for Psychotherapy in Bellmore, New York, a
common tendency is to lump all sources of stress together into
one package instead of separating them, resulting in feeling
overwhelmed. Many people expend their energy trying harder
and harder to attain goals that are just not realistic. The result:
more stress. It is important to set up reasonable standards you
can live up to.

This may mean making changes in your lifestyle to reduce your stress level. Some of the following suggestions might seem obvious, but so are speed limit signs, warnings on cigarette packages, advice from Ann Landers and curfews in dormitories—just because we know what's right doesn't mean we always adhere to the rules. But where there's life, there's hope—maybe this time it'll sink in. (You do wear your seatbelt, put on suntan lotion and recycle your soda cans, don't you?)

Coping with stress on a long-term basis will be less exhausting if you:

1) Set limits. Consider ways you can slow down or lighten your schedule. What can you leave for the weekend or delegate to someone else? Crossing two tasks off your "to do" list may make a difference in the stress you feel. Don't overburden yourself with more than what is realistic. Don't try to do it all.

2) Ask for help. You can't do everything yourself. Overload is probably partly responsible for your high stress level. Swallow your pride and ask for help from anyone whose support you can count on.

3) Learn to say no. Saying no doesn't mean that you're not competent. It's a better decision than overcommitting yourself. For all the yesses you give in your hectic life, when demands are excessive it's okay to say no to your children, spouse, friends, neighbors, relatives, community agencies, and even your boss.

4) Plan in advance to avoid stressful situations. If you know what is most likely to affect you, you can plan accordingly. If arriving late to an appointment gets you stressed, leave earlier to allow more travel time. If you feel your body tense at the thought of driving in traffic, try arranging your schedule to travel at off-peak times.

For Kim, 30, an art director for a public relations firm, coming home at the end of a long day to a whining, demanding two-year-old was an unyielding source of stress. She couldn't wait to spend time with her daughter Marci, but she desperately needed a few minutes by herself to unwind before sitting down on the floor to color by number and build cities from blocks. A fellow working mom suggested a plan that has made a world of difference. A late afternoon trip to a nearby park has become a daily ritual for Marci and her babysitter—leaving an empty apartment for Kim when she arrives home from work. With no pressure to be "on" the minute she opens the door, Kim has 20 minutes of alone time to change her clothes, read the mail and check messages. By the time Marci returns, her mom is ready and waiting for her.

5) Set aside one time during the day, for no more than 30 minutes, for a "Worry Period." If you find your mind wandering at other times during the day with worries— the fight you had in the morning with your daughter, your mother-in-law's high blood pressure, the upcoming business trip, the decision over whether to move—write them down on a piece of paper and save them for your worry period. Use that time to analyze your worries, and decide which are beyond your control and therefore useless to worry about and which are situations to be dealt with. Promise yourself the time to come up with a logical plan to deal with those concerns.[2]

6) Make time for activities that give you pleasure. No matter how overloaded your schedule is, don't eliminate the hobbies and interests that help make the rest of your life worthwhile.

It is vital to break the stress cycle with an activity you find soothing. It may be *physical*—going for a walk or a jog; *mental*—doing a crossword puzzle or reading a book of poems; *sensory*—listening to music; or *social*—calling a friend. Anything that takes you outside your routine and gives you pleasure can effectively break the stress cycle.

Energy Begets Energy

In our culture where work is equated with income and income is equated with happiness, it's hard to remember that simple pleasures can rejuvenate the soul. We have to take responsibility for our stressed-out selves and work on ways to rev up limp energy levels, for often it is the lack of energy, rather than the lack of time, skills or desire, that limits our enjoyment of life. There are no "shoulds" here—only simple, inexpensive, easy-to-implement suggestions designed to add pleasure to your day. If there's time to change the oil in your car and fold the laundry, then there's time to inject a little whimsy into your schedule as well.

1) Choose a fun aerobic activity (like bicycling, dancing or walking)—not for its fat-reducing, heart-strengthening benefits but for its ability to activate the chemicals in the brain that can improve your mood.

2) Model your behavior after a ten-year-old—eat a chocolate bar in the late afternoon, sing along with the radio, get down and dirty with the kids, work hardest when you feel like it (late morning is most people's optimum time) and do mindless, repetitive tasks when your body slumps.

3) Treat boredom as the enemy and defeat it by doing the same old thing in a new way (trade chores for the day, watch the news on a different channel, try preparing a brand-new dish for dinner).

4) Visit the health food store and discover a whole new world of holistic stress busters, from herbal teas to vitamins to natural bath oils.

5) Con a loved one into giving you a massage—a guaranteed energy booster. Then return the favor.

6) Be kind to your feet. Take off your shoes and soak those hardworking digits in a soothing tub. You'll feel the benefits right up into your neck and shoulders.

7) Laugh. We know that laughter has been documented to have a wondrous healing effect. Whether it's movies or the comics, tickling or giggling, laughing is a great defense against a demanding world. Remember, he who laughs, lasts!

8) Keep in mind that what you're feeling is curable and preventable. Be aware that the power to make yourself better is yours, and in the scheme of things, learning to use it is not the hardest thing you do in a week.

According to Dr. Lipner, after 45 to 50 minutes of working or studying, you will probably begin to lose your concentration and your retention will wane. If you take a ten-minute break, you are more likely to feel rejuvenated and be receptive to continuing whatever you were working on. Don't regard taking a break as losing time. Once your concentration goes, you start reading the same material over and over again. If you continue without a break, anxiety levels mount and you begin to lose efficiency.

"I'm guilty," confesses Carole (the school superintendent introduced in Chapter 1). "If no one reminded me, I'd go nonstop from 7:30 a.m. until 5 p.m. and never eat lunch. Fortunately, my secretary comes in midday and pushes me out the door. I usually go into town and pick up a sandwich, then browse for a few minutes in a local card store. By the time I return to the office, it's almost like beginning a new day."

Dr. Lipner cautions that when breaking the stress cycle it is important to choose activities that are soothing and nonstressful themselves. "Many people think they relax by playing golf. But on the golf course they get so frustrated and upset when they play poorly that they wind up not reducing stress but rather adding more to their lives. They'd be better off working!"

Ron, a 32-year-old electrician, can attest to that. "For two years, every Wednesday night I went bowling with a few of the guys. We all work hard and this was our night out—a couple of hours of physical activity and male bonding. We each threw a few dollars into the pot and set up a minitournament. At first I thought it was a great idea. But on the nights I didn't bowl well I came home in the worst mood."

"He was a grump," agrees Ron's wife, Barbara. "Finally I asked him why he was doing this. When he told me it was to relax, I cracked up in his face. If this was how he acted after relaxing, I'd hate to be in the same state with him after he did something stressful!"

EXERCISE—THE VALIUM OF THE 90s

Nothing you introduce into your life can break up and dissipate stress as efficiently as finding and implementing the right exercise program. "Short of modifying the underlying conditions of your life (leaving your job, giving away the kids...) exercise on a regular basis is the quickest way to find physical relief from the negative symptoms of stress. Whether you choose an activity that's long and repetitive (running or swimming) or one that engages concentration as well as activating the body (racquetball or tennis) will depend on your personal preference, but any choice or combination of choices will release stress," says Dr. Havlichek, director of the Institute for Psychosomatic Research in Roslyn, New York. "The Chinese and the Japanese have known this for years. They start the day at industrial settings, factories and schools with a required series of exercises that inoculate them, at least for a few hours, against the pressures that lay ahead. A fit body adapts more efficiently to stress by pumping out smaller amounts of the fight-or-flight hormones. These exercises create a self-centering that increases energy, loosens muscles and provides a powerful sedative to combat the day's stressors."

The reward after exercise is relaxation and peace of mind. "The most relaxed I feel all day is after a half hour on the stair master at lunchtime," says Jane, 35, an insurance broker lucky enough to work for a corporation that built a gym in the building for its employees two years ago. "Aside from feeling noble about giving up half of my lunch hour, I actually feel my body is purged, cleaned out of all the jitter demons. I swear, at 11:45 my knee is jumping up and down under my desk, for whatever reason, at 90 miles per hour. After lunch my whole body language is different. And exercising midday works great for me. I feel the benefits right up through dinnertime."

"I'm so preoccupied with trying to serve five masters simultaneously that if I didn't work out, I don't think I'd ever know what it feels like to be totally relaxed," says Bob, 31, an account executive with an advertising firm. "I'm always so driven to accomplish that it's very hard for me to just 'be.' All my friends grew up the same way—we taught ourselves to be knowledgeable about wines and computers and politics and cinema. But I don't know if one of us spent any time learning what it is that makes us feel most relaxed."

WHO ARE YOU GOING TO CALL? STRESSBUSTERS!

Then there are those unplanned and unexpected times when stress just attacks. It may strike at the office, in your car or while waiting on line at the supermarket. Your fingers feel cold; your palms feel wet. Your temples start thumping; your lower back aches. It might not happen often but its symptoms are so upsetting because their unpredictability leaves us without tools at our disposal to fight back. At these moments when anxiety threatens to ruin your day, these short-term "stressbusters" can quickly lower your stress level.

At home

1) Take a long shower or herbal bath—even ten minutes can be truly magic for frazzled nerves.

2) Take time out for a treat. Read a magazine; watch a TV show that has no redeeming value; call a friend to catch up on the latest gossip; read sections of your newspaper you never have time to read.

Away from home

3) Stuck in traffic? Carry a tape of your favorite music and pop it in. Have you tried listening to a book on tape? If you can't concentrate and feel that you're wasting precious time, a car phone may be an appropriate stress-buster. (Installing a car phone, however, will take away your quiet moments alone. You might be able to knock off a call or two, but consider the trade-off—you will open yourself up to the questions, demands and requests of the world beyond your windshield. If you do decide to get a car phone, be cautious about giving out your number!) Finally, learn to remove yourself mentally from the bottleneck. Let your mind take you to another time, another place—a favorite vacation spot or a recent pleasurable activity. Enjoy the memories. Or, use your mind for something productive: Plan the guest list for an upcoming party; decide what you have to pack for a business trip or vacation.

4) Trapped in a waiting room or on line at the bank? Always carry something with you that's enjoyable to read or do. It may be a good novel, a book of crossword puzzles or even a needlepoint project.

5) Delayed on a plane or stuck overnight on a business trip? Plan ahead with back-up systems in place: a goody bag of munchies for travel, an extra set of clothes for unplanned delays.

Anywhere

6) Meditate. In your office, at home, even sitting in your car in the quiet corner of a parking lot. Close your eyes, shut out the day. Picture yourself lying on a beach, in a hammock, any place you associate with peacefulness. Breathe deeply, and let your mind relax for ten minutes. Remember, this is a gift you've earned.

Even Corporations Show Compassion

Twenty years ago the last person in the world you could run to for relief from the stresses and strains of maintaining a three-career relationship would be your boss. And the bigger the business, the less your concerns would matter. Today things are beginning to turn around—hopefully marking the beginning of a new time of understanding, when companies realize that it's good business to lend a hand to employees whose work is suffering because of stress.

When the pressures of juggling three careers begin to affect performance, many corporations are choosing to deal with their employees' emotional turmoil rather than replace them. Corporate America's hard-boiled image is softening. Employee assistance programs, or EAPs, were originally set up as a way to help employees overcome their alcohol and substance abuse problems. Today they address a wide range of psychological, social and emotional problems that interfere with employee performance.

Generally, EAP counselors assess the problem and then refer workers to either a psychologist, a drug rehabilitation center or a marital counselor. In some programs, EAP professionals work with supervisory people within the company and teach them how to identify particular problems and even run workshops on common emotional issues. Aside from generating good will, these attempts to alleviate the negative effects of stress make good business sense. They minimize the expense of firing and recruiting new staff, which is much more costly than helping employees recover their balance.[3] And since we're all familiar with our minds' cunning ability to make our bodies sick, it also saves money to resolve problems before serious physical symptoms appear.

Among work-family programs offered by companies surveyed in the Corporate Reference Guide Survey by Families and Work Institute, EAPs ranked second in prevalence (part-time work schedules came in first). Eighty-six percent of the 160 firms interviewed offered confidential mental health counseling and assistance to their employees. Another 11 companies were considering implementing these programs in the near future. Most of the EAPs in the companies studied reached well beyond substance abuse assistance. They served employees by dealing with a variety of personal, family and work-family problems. Overall, the annual usage rate averaged about six percent of the work force.[4]

If you work for a company that has an employee assistance program, take advantage of it. Help is help, whether the motivation is derived from a sincere attempt to better the state of your personal well-being—or from a more self-centered concern about lessening the disruption your problems may be causing the organization.

GIVE YOURSELF A BREAK—BE KIND TO YOUR BODY

We are the generation who grew up believing if we ate our Wheaties we'd become Champions, and if we made sandwiches with Wonder Bread our bodies would grow strong in 12 ways. As working adults we eat on the run, often with a diet too high in fat and sugar. We don't make the time to get a good night's sleep, and we say we're too busy to exercise faithfully. We're not that old and we look okay, so we assume we're safe in neglecting our physical well-being—until we realize that the alarming statistics about obesity, alcoholism, high blood pressure and heart disease apply to young, good-looking us. We stop for a moment and promise ourselves to be kinder to our bodies. None of the following hints will be new to you, but maybe seeing them in yet another context will motivate you to take heed. For people as accomplished as we are, as committed to doing a good job on all fronts, we must get over seeing ourselves as immortal and stop thinking of basic diet and health maintenance information as boring and irrelevant.

Dr. Stuart Dolgin, a fellow of the American College of Gastroenterology with a private practice in Merrick, New York, offers the following commonsense (but not-to-be-taken-for-granted) advice for keeping your body healthy. It will go a long way in helping to keep stress in check.

- Avoid excess salt in your diet. Salt tends to raise blood pressure, which can lead to heart attacks.

- Reduce your consumption of saturated fats. Fat in your diet increases weight gain; and it increases the level of cholesterol in your blood, which is associated with heart disease.

- Instead, increase your intake of low-fat foods: fruits, vegetables, whole grains, fish and poultry instead of red meat. Evidence suggests that eating foods low in fat reduces the risk of colon cancer.

- Exercise regularly—worth another mention. This is one of the most effective ways to control weight. Although difficult to document, most experts agree that the process of exercise also helps to discharge energy and release stress. The ideal exercise program is some form of aerobic exercise that stimulates your heart rate three to four times a week for a minimum of 20 minutes each time.

YOU CAN LEARN TO RELAX!

Many Three-Career Couples feel guilt if they are not accomplishing their goal, even if that goal happens to be relaxation. They try to pursue it with the same aggressive attitude they bring to other tasks in their lives. But the secret to getting the best results from relaxation is to stop striving and *just be.*

- Do not be afraid to try something new. Choose activities you really enjoy—not those you think other people want you to pursue. Knitting or fishing might not be as trendy as hip hop or rollerblading, but the end result—personal satisfaction—is as cutting edge as they come.

- Explore and discover those things that give you pleasure. Try to devote 30 minutes or so every day to something that makes you feel good. We know you don't have that half hour easily accessible, but what are the other 23½ hours about if not trying to get the most out of this twirl around planet Earth?

- Be as committed to relaxation as you are to your work. Don't underestimate its importance. Convince yourself that relaxation is essential for your physical and mental well-being. And if that doesn't work, convince yourself that a happier, less tense you will more easily survive the day.

- Try some mental exercises to create a sense of peace and tranquility in body and mind. Find a comfortable position and close your eyes. Concentrate on relaxing successive sets of muscles from the tips of your toes to the muscles in your forehead and neck. Deeply and gently inhale to the count of four through your nose, and exhale to the count of four through your mouth. As you exhale, say the word "one" silently to yourself. Repeat inhaling and exhaling, and repeat the word "one" silently for five minutes. Remember to allow distracting thoughts to drift on by. Relaxation will occur at its own pace. As you begin to stir, count backward from three. At the count of two, open your eyes. At the count of one, bring yourself to awareness. Get up slowly, feeling refreshed.

Simple exercises like this one have been popularly touted as quick, easy stress relievers since the 70s. Try incorporating them into your routine for a week and see how the mind can unkink, loosen and slow down a body headed for trouble.[5]

"One of the most relaxing times for me is early morning, before anyone in the house is up," says Peggy, an office manager and mother of three. "Since I started working a regular nine to five job, I've begun to wake up one hour earlier in order to have time for myself while it's still quiet. I never thought I'd ever actually admit that I like getting up at 5:30, but it's so peaceful at that hour. By six I've had my first cup of coffee, and I'm awake enough to start my morning exercise. I either ride my stationary bike or put in a Jane Fonda tape and follow her workout. It gets me going and energizes me. My husband thinks I'm out of my mind, but for me this early morning routine really works. By seven I'm showered and ready to wake the family and get started on the day."

PARTNERS OR ADVERSARIES?

"I have enough stress in my life," says Phil, a 39-year-old pediatrician. "The last thing I need is more tension between Donna and me when I finally get home from the office. We don't mean to push each other's buttons, but too often it just happens. I say 'Chinese takeout,' she says 'Italian.' I say 'You look tired,' she gets insulted. If I forget to tell her I'm on call and she's made plans for us to go out with friends, she gets furious."

Donna, a 37-year-old matrimonial attorney, agrees. "We need about six months alone together, to chill out and remember the way it used to be when we lived with manageable stress. It's hard to believe that time ever existed."

Stress felt by Three-Career Couples is often an outgrowth of the way in which they have arranged their lives. According to Dr. Lipner, the most important indicator of a good marriage is sharing common goals and values.

"If you're not pulling in the same direction there will be a lot of resentment along the way, with a reluctant passenger throwing roadblocks because he or she doesn't want to move that way."

To manage stress as partners:

1) Make time for each other. Set up a designated time (or times) during the week to spend together, without distractions or interruptions. Go out for lunch or dinner, or meet at home at a time when you won't be interrupted or distracted. Take the phone off the hook, put on the answering machine or have someone inform callers that you cannot be disturbed. Try being creative: Meet at a hotel, motel, bar, health club, any place where you can find time alone, just for each other.

2) Assess and reassess. On a continuous basis discuss your goals and expectations—for yourselves, your relationship, your family. Are your standards realistic? Are you spending your energy in ways that are appropriate for you? Are you moving in the direction that satisfies you?

3) Share your stress. It helps to talk about your concerns and worries. You can reduce some of the pressure that comes from feeling overwhelmed by sharing your vulnerability with your partner.

"When Stan told me that while he's at work he worries about Lisa in the day care center, I started to cry," confesses Rita, a 34-year-old English teacher. "There was such a sense of sweet relief to know that I wasn't the only one who worries about her, that he shares my anxiety—that we really are partners."

Chapter 9, "I Miss You; Fax Me a Hug," deals with these issues in greater detail. We need to constantly remember that the problems created by the three-career lifestyle are not ours to solve alone. For better or worse, partners are in this together, and we'd be foolish not to take advantage of the source of support lying next to us each night.

DON'T SAY THE G WORD!

A chapter about stress would not be complete without a discussion of the G word. Ever-present guilt, a cousin to stress and anxiety, friend of frustration and exhaustion, is in a category by itself.

We feel guilty that we rush off to work and miss the best years of our children's lives; we feel guilty that we're not concentrating enough on the biggest project of our career because we're worried about our family; we feel guilty that we haven't had a home-cooked meal in a week, that we haven't had the in-laws over for dinner for the past month, that we missed the school play, that we've missed exercise class for the last two weeks. And we feel guilty that we waste so much time on such an irrational, self-defeating emotion.

Women may not have the monopoly on guilt, but they surely control more of its stock! Most would agree: Whatever they're doing, it isn't enough.

Men feel less guilt than women, says Dr. Kimmel, a nationally recognized expert on gender and sexuality, because the existing state of their lives tells them that they *are* less guilty. What they feel reflects the roles they have set up with the woman as the primary nurturer, caregiver, orchestrator of child care and housework. As men, they are supposed to be out working. Being a breadwinner and a father is synonymous with being a man. There is no sense of incompatibility and little, if any, guilt.

For women, the side effect of this dual pursuit is gnawing, omnipresent and chronic guilt. The job description (demanding competence and compassion in a hundred areas) is so daunting that to even attempt to do it successfully part-time is a courageous act. Because there are as many books in the library chronicling outstanding practitioners of this career/woman/ wife/mother/own person with no wrinkles, a tight abdomen and great kids as there are books on sumptuous 200-calorie fat-free desserts, women often feel as if they're doomed to always fall short of satisfying their own expectations.

There is some good news on the horizon, however. A 1992 Gallup Poll discovered that 58 percent of working mothers feel their personal work situation doesn't affect the quality of their mothering.[6] Among moms who feel their work situation does have an impact on their children, 14 percent feel it makes them better, not worse, mothers.[7]

Nevertheless, many parents overbuy, overindulge and overprotect. "I know it's wrong," admits Stacy, 30, and mother of four-year-old Brittany. "But I feel so guilty that I'm away so much I tend to let things slide that I wouldn't if I weren't working. So what's the big deal if she eats in the den instead of the kitchen? When she begs to stay up until ten o'clock because she wants to spend time with Mommy and Daddy, how can I say no? I've seen the disapproving look on my best friend's face when she's over for dinner, but she can't really understand because she doesn't work full time. I can't help it; this is how I cope with not being home more."

It's a form of vanity to believe that anyone can change hats as often as we do and never commit a fashion faux pas. Taking the easy way out, wanting gratification in all parts of your life, even putting your needs before those of others, are not offenses that deserve to be punished by a lifetime of recriminations. Overcoming guilt is a learned process. The more you practice, the more convincing it feels.

■ If you think your guilt is justified, change the situation that caused it. If, for example, you have been negligent in seeing your in-laws, arrange to invite them over. If you have serious doubts about your choice of child care, come up with a new decision that makes you feel more comfortable.

If, however, you feel that you are doing the best you can—

■ Acknowledge that the difficult situations children face are not necessarily related to their parents working. No matter how perfect a parent you are, your children will have problems at different times while growing up. There will be fights with friends, disappointing grades and broken promises till the end of time, regardless of how you spend your day.

■ Accept your strengths and weaknesses and forgive yourself for not being "perfect." What kind of message is a parent sending who demands such impossibly high standards for herself or himself? You'll all wind up sipping Maalox cocktails.

■ Remind yourself that you have the right to enjoy your achievements. This should be so easy, but it's not.

■ Cast out any lingering guilt by repeating:
1) I do the best I can at home and at work.
2) I'm not a Superhero. I can't do everything.
3) When I'm happy, so is my family.

Iris, a 32-year-old wife, mother and nurse, can't get into bed each night without coming face-to-face with the sign her husband made for her. The message in neon letters on a black background says: "Guilt Is a Wasted Emotion." It is taped to the wall next to her side of their bed, directly over the phone.

"She can't miss it," chuckles her husband, Bob. "I was tired of hearing all the time about how guilty she felt. Over everything—the kids, me, the house, her parents, our friends. She used up so much time and energy feeling guilty that she was always exhausted! And where did it get her? Nowhere! I'd always tell her, 'If you want to do something differently, do it. If not, that's okay, then live with it.' In our house we've dubbed guilt the G word, and it is not permitted. End of discussion."

SUMMING IT UP

Like many Three-Career Couples you've probably grown accustomed to living with days that leave you feeling that the best you can do is not quite good enough.

But with greater understanding of what causes stress and how your body responds to it—and a willingness to make some changes—you can make a difference in your stress life—both individually and as a couple.

As a "new" Three-Career Couple you can try to uncomplicate your lives by:

- Doing everything possible—and no more. "I'll pick up some fresh vegetables on the way home from work before I drive the car pool. Maybe I can squeeze in the shoe-maker—and make up that extra set of keys. And maybe not; tomorrow's another day."

- Recognizing symptoms of stress and what it takes to push the stress buttons. "It's the sixteenth week of the football season, there are nine days till Christmas and the annual report is due in three days. This Sunday headache is defi-nitely *not* a brain tumor."

- Planning accordingly to avoid stressful situations whenever possible. "If you're flying into the airport 8 p.m. Thanks-giving eve, take a cab. Come in a day earlier and I'll be there to pick you up with bells on."

- Taking time to relax—planning time for exercise, relax-ation, diversion and stimulation. Because it feels good doesn't mean it's not necessary. Because you might have fun doesn't mean it's a frill.

■ Learning, by practice, to overcome feelings of guilt. "It's not my fault if *you're* unhappy; it's only my fault if *I'm* unhappy."

■ Analyzing support networks and asking for help when needed. What kind of friend would you be if you didn't sometimes allow your friends the pleasure of making your life easier?

And as partners—

■ Listing the causes of your discomfort and working together to alleviate stress.

■ Investigating what can be done individually and as a team.

■ Seeing if working hours can be altered and/or if people can be hired (a babysitter, a cleaning person, someone to cut the grass, maybe even people for pick-up and delivery services) to ease the burden.

■ Taking time out—a week would be great, a day is better than nothing—just to think about the changes to be made to ensure that you won't be back in the very same place next month.

IT'S 7:30 A.M. AND I'M ALREADY AN HOUR LATE!
Managing Time Efficiently

Time goes, you say? Alas Time stays; we go.
Henry Austin Dobson

Exactly where is the bank that stores all the extra minutes and fragments of hours we're so bent on saving? If we can't withdraw them when we need them, we should at least be entitled to live some weeks or even months longer when our time runs out. The busier our lives are, the more we're encouraged not to waste one second. Unfortunately, some time management books advise us not to fritter away our day doing one task at a time. "Test your child's spelling while you're cooking dinner." Yeah, right. "Make up your supermarket shopping list while you're driving to work." Sure thing. And why not do your isometric exercises while watching the news and folding the laundry? Why not? Because our minds and bodies were not made to work efficiently for very long at such a pace.

"My life is so hectic that there is no way I could sit still long enough for my nails to dry after polishing them," says Marcia, 29, a suburban mother of two who runs a stationery business from her home. "My solution? Cutting holes in my gloves so my nails would dry while I do my daily three-mile run. This time-saving hint works brilliantly for most of the year. I'm still working on a solution for the summer months when my nails bubble from the heat!"

This obsessive concern with making use of every spare minute is not unusual. "I never leave the house without my filofax, a newspaper, a book or at the very least a blank pad," says Alan, 40, a psychologist whose entire working life is inflexibly run by the clock. "The other day my son asked me to drive him to the drugstore to pick up a prescription. I ran out of the house with just my wallet, parked outside the store and waited for him to come out. The pharmacist was backed up and said it would take another ten minutes. My son found a friend to pass the time. But I sat, in agony, without anything to do. I'm embarrassed to say that I was so agitated I didn't even think of turning on the radio and listening to some music. My wife, who knows better than anyone how crazy I am, got me this poster that hangs in my office. It just says, 'Life is what happens to you when you're making other plans.' Sometimes I feel that's all I do—make plans to make life easier sometime in the future."

"There's not a woman I know who's personally familiar with the concept of 'spare time,' says Joan, 26, a high school science teacher. 'In-between time' is spent making phone calls, doing errands, planning menus, shopping for clothes or arranging car pools. I'm forever picking up a constantly changing, yet always the same, 'few things.'"

According to Toni Liebman, former nursery school director, author and parent educator, you have to stop what you're doing and re-evaluate. Ask yourself what are the things in your life that are most important. Then look at how you're spending your time. If you find that where you're spending the most time is not on what's really most important, it's time for a rearrangement.

For instance, if you find that you're spending too much time grumbling about the state of the kids' rooms, the tarnished candlesticks and the messy den, you might consider looking away a bit more. View it as a raising of your tolerance level rather than a lowering of tidiness standards. Change is difficult, but waking up to the same jam-packed, ultimately unsatisfying day over and over may be harder.

SETTING GOALS

Most of our stress about time occurs when we spend too much of it far afield from the most important areas in life. It's a good idea to review the goals most important to you—for your family, career achievement, leisure time, personal development, etc. Make sure they are measurable (*not* "I just want to be happy"), realistic (*not* wanting to beat Michael Jordan at basketball), attainable (maybe *not* a three-month trip around the world) and broken down into manageably sized pieces. Then put them in order of importance. Estimate the time you spend on each one. Is time, as you spend it, proportionate to the priority of each goal? If not, it's time to cut down on the activities that add little to the quality of your life.

We all spend too much time on mundane chores that tend to crowd out what's life-affirming, simple and most important, like playing with the kids or having a quiet dinner alone. Before beginning a task we should question how essential it is and whether it needs to be done immediately. Often the task is completed because we're acting out of habit, not because it's high priority. What's the real urgency, for instance, in racing to make

Time Mismanagement Quiz

How many of the following thoughts have passed through your mind this week?

1) I should be able to accomplish more in a day.
2) Time is money; don't people know that?
3) I wish he'd speak faster.
4) When did the leaves fall off (change color, turn green)?
5) Why is it that every line I wait on is the one that moves the slowest?
6) There's no way I'm going to get everything done.
7) I wish I could trust someone else to do this job, but I know it would be done wrong.
8) Everyone's taking advantage of my competence, and I'm doing more than my fair share.
9) If this guy doesn't drive any faster, I'm going to ram into him.
10) I feel frustrated, overwhelmed and out of control from the demands in my life.

Think about the circumstances that brought up these thoughts. Be conscious of how your behavior contributes to the unreasonably heavy load you're carrying. What is it that's so pressing, so life-and-death important, that makes a 30-second red light or a six-minute bank line seem so torturous? How crucial is squeezing in time to return the library books? Worth the damage that the state you work yourself into does to your equilibrium? Doubtful. And what do you know that is so esoteric, so intellectually intricate that a gifted person like you could not explain to someone else so that he or she could do it? Not much. Once again, it's vanity to believe that only you, stressed, overbooked, tired you, has the key to understanding the universe.

If you can convince yourself to implement some of the suggestions provided in this chapter, we guarantee you'll lessen the number of times you feel pushed beyond your physical and emotional limits.

the beds each morning? Certainly it's a job that can be delegated, done later or skipped altogether.

Dr. Donald A. Tubesing, author of *Kicking Your Stress Habits,* talks about establishing priorities. "Divide your tasks into three categories: essential, important and trivial—and forget about the trivial. Hire others, including your own children, to do the tasks that can be farmed out. Learn to say no when you're asked to do something that overloads your time or stress budget or diverts you from what you consider most important. Be satisfied with a less-than-perfect job if the alternative is not getting a job done at all. Identify the activities themselves rather than your performance or what rewards they will bring."[1]

ADDING ORDER TO A LIST-LESS LIFE

We probably all know disorganized people who live on the edge, with a constant sense of impending disaster. They're always minutes away from something going wrong, but they don't know what, when or how. They never feel on top of the demands of their lives—because they don't plan ahead. If we don't plan, we can't predict, prepare for or cope with the future. It's the act of deciding what we want to do and how we will go about doing it that protects us from that awful "we're running as fast as we can but we're never going to catch up" feeling. The single most important tool we have for breaking out of this cycle is taking regular time every day to sit down and plan. For those of you allergic to lists, we apologize. This chapter is chock-full of them! We believe in their ability to expedite information, and we hope you'll see them as useful tools rather than dictatorial orders.

"Both Ron and I are list-addicted people," says Barbara 28. "We keep our separate daily lists for our work life—one half of them is day-to-day things to do, the other half is by the week. I keep a separate list on a magnetized pad on the refrigerator for house- and kid-related chores. We've learned to be careful and not assign each other a list of things to do. There's something very annoying about following a series of tasks generated by someone else. That's why it never works with the kids. On the weekends we keep a list together of errands, appointments and phone calls that have to be made. We both get so much satisfaction crossing things off when they're done that we've been known to fight over who has the honor! And sick as it sounds, if we do something that wasn't on the list, we add it for the pure pleasure of seeing how much we've accomplished at the end of the day. I've even awakened in the middle of the night and called my answering machine at work to remind myself of a few more things to add. When we entertain, it really gets complicated. There's a 'week before' list, a 'day before' list and a 'day of' list. Recounting all this I know sounds obsessive, but it's not harmful and it's the only way for us."

The Daily "To Do" List

Here are a few simple rules to follow when making up an efficient, stress-reducing, time-managing list.

1) Make a new list at the start of every day. You can add yesterday's leftovers if there are any.

2) Try to limit the list to around six items. We know sometimes that's impossible, but it's important to be realistic and aware of the limitations of your time. You can always add more if you have hours left over with no tasks to fill them! The purpose of doing this is to organize a more successful you, not to set yourself up for failure and frustration.

3) Rank the items in order of importance. You must get to the dentist; you don't have to fold the laundry.

4) Complete the tasks in that order, except for those that are time related.

5) Allow yourself a time cushion between entries. Again, don't overschedule.

6) Include fun stuff, too, so that a look at the list is not all drudgery and difficult tasks.[2]

───────────

"I recently took a seminar on time management for business managers, and for the first time in my life I learned to schedule things into my day and make them happen," says Burt, 42, and the owner of several restaurants. "I keep a list of what I have to do—an A list of the most important things and a B list of the less important tasks—up till noon. Then I schedule in a lunch hour break; if I didn't write it down, I'd never take the time. From 3 until 4 p.m. I schedule in an hour to leave and work out. Then I have things that must be done by the end of the day. It really works. When it's in front of me in black and white I feel more in control and things get done more efficiently. Now my wife and I schedule in time for each other on our monthly calendars. Even though that was just as important as errands and work-related stuff, it was often neglected. Getting into making lists gets you to think about how you're really spending your life."

THERE IS MORE THAN ONE RIGHT WAY

We do too much, but it all needs doing. We need breathing space, but we don't know where or how to find it. Skills in time management have become essential in our lives—for getting through a day, a week, a season. While we all face the challenges of stretching the minutes and using time most effectively, coping styles vary as much as the individuals themselves. It works for some to get up first in the morning—for others it works to sleep another ten minutes. Some have every task of the day written down with the time it'll be done—others pseudo-wing it. It is important to remember that there is not just one right way to manage time. What works for one may be ineffective for another.

Leslie and Roberta are coowners of a busy children's boutique. Both in their mid-thirties, the partners share much in common. They are both energetic and creative, productive and efficient, yet when it comes to their strategies for scheduling and structuring their days, they are worlds apart. Leslie is up and in the shop by 7:30 a.m. to complete her share of the paperwork before store hours; Roberta prefers to use her lunch hour relaxing with a sandwich in their tiny office while she does filing and other necessary paperwork. During Leslie's lunch break she dashes out to take care of her Third Career errands; Roberta, on the other hand, waits until evening and takes her children with her for family errands. Leslie is a compulsive list keeper who gets great satisfaction from crossing off each daily task as she completes it; Roberta, by contrast, gets nervous at the sight of a list and keeps her "to do's" in her head. For business phone calls, Leslie has a designated time every afternoon, while Roberta makes a few at a time and spreads the dreaded task out over the day.

Amazingly, the difference in Leslie's and Roberta's approach to time management hasn't interfered with their compatibility. They are, in fact, amused by their different styles of coping and enjoy teasing each other about their "eccentric" habits.

While Leslie uses her lunch hour for errands and Roberta for routine office tasks, Jane, 25, the insurance broker who works out in her company's gym, wouldn't give up her exercise time for anything less than an emergency. Marty, 41, a stockbroker, commutes by train to work, giving himself an hour each way to read the newspaper and catch up on paperwork. Steve, 43, in the same firm, prefers the solitude in his car. Having discovered novels on cassette, he actually looks forward to his commute and has conquered his frustration at not having time for books.

DEFINING YOUR OWN WORK STYLE

Before attempting to get your world into more manageable order, take a moment to answer these questions and analyze what your particular work style is. It's amazing how much we know about the sad habits of those around us, and how little we know about our own. Written lists or mental lists? Lunch hour for exercise, errands or eating? Grocery shopping at night or on Sunday? To develop a plan that uses your time most efficiently, first assess your personal schedule, priorities and lifestyle.

1) What time of day does your energy level peak? Are you sharpest in the morning? Or does late afternoon bring out the best of your productivity and creativity?

2) Are you a creature of habit who prefers the same routine every day, or do you enjoy varying your schedule?

3) Do you work better with a daily plan of goals to be accomplished, or do you prefer to make your schedule over a week?

4) What is your maximum concentration time? For how long can you work on a project or activity before becoming restless, distracted or bored?

5) Do you prefer to tackle major tasks in one block of time or to break them up into several shorter sessions? Would you rather clean up your whole desk in one morning or tackle one drawer at a time? Write an annual report in one sitting or concentrate on one page each day?

6) Are there natural breaks in your day that you can use to switch gears and change activities?

7) Do you take a lunch break at the same time every day? Do you use part of your lunchtime for anything other than eating?

8) Would you prefer to fit in errands (haircut, grocery shopping, post office, bank, dry cleaners, etc.) after work, on weekends or during short breaks during the day?

After answering these questions, you can determine your individual coping style and establish your personal plan to best manage your precious time.

Lucille, a 30-year-old office manager, after analyzing her own work style, learned something she had never realized before: the relief of getting the most unpleasant things over early in the day. "Now I pick the worst thing I have to do each day and schedule it early in the morning so I can forget about it," she explains. "Thursday is Linen Day in my house; I *hate* changing sheets. So I get up 20 minutes earlier every Thursday and get it over with. Yesterday I had to call the water company because we had a dispute over the last bill. So I made that the day's dreaded chore and called first thing in the morning. If there's something I have to do at the office—like reprimand an employee or come up with a new lunch schedule that I know everyone will complain about—those are the things that get put first on the list. When they're finished, I don't have to think about another awful chore until tomorrow!"

Implementing your plan

In developing your own time management policy, bear in mind these helpful hints:

- Use your highest energy time of day for priority tasks.
- Use more sluggish times for less intense activities, like returning routine phone calls, filing, sorting mail, etc.
- Build in a separate quiet time in your day, to be used for work that requires thoughtful planning and creativity. Try to make it free of phone calls and interruptions.
- Use natural breaks—lunchtime, coffee breaks, exercise hour—to go from one project to another.
- If you keep a daily plan, keep it visible all day long; it will help you stay on target.
- Performing the same tasks at the same time of day reduces the time it takes to get focused on each task.

- Keep a separate list of quick "to do's" that can be completed in five minutes or less. When you have a short block of free time, refer to your list and take care of one of your "quickie" tasks.

- Schedule in even obvious activities so you'll be sure not to forget to do them. Don't give yourself an opportunity to eliminate lunch or exercise—no matter how busy you may be. If they're on your schedule, you'll be compelled to make time for them.[3]

TEAM TIME MANAGEMENT IS ALSO A MUST

Time management planning, while personal and individual, must also take your partner into consideration. For Ellen and Bruce, both 34, scheduling time after work at the park with 18-month-old Chris on a take-turns basis has been helpful in allowing each to have time alone and time with their son.

"In Florida it stays light late, so we're lucky," Ellen explains. "When Bruce and I get home from work, we're both dying to get our hands on Chris, but we also need time to unwind. Since I get home a half hour before Bruce, I take the first shift—Chris and I head to the park for some bonding time before Daddy gets home. Meanwhile, Bruce comes home, sets the table, changes into a pair of shorts and meets us at the park. Then it's my time to go home, take a shower, start dinner and put up my feet for a few minutes. Bruce and I have our evenings once Chris is asleep. That hour after we get home used to be Chris's cranky time. Now that he's so happy at the park, we have added the bonus of avoiding the witching hour. This change in routine has made coming home from work infinitely more pleasurable."

Team time management makes provisions for:

- Scheduling in time alone for you and your partner.

- Dividing Third-Career responsibilities—driving car pools,

grocery shopping, doctor appointments—and scheduling them into your own daily plans.

- Keeping in touch with each other to avoid the confusion, misunderstandings and communication gaps that lead to the same activity being done twice, or worse, not done at all.

Firsthand testimony for the need to touch base comes from Sharon, a 31-year-old art dealer, who admits that she and her husband Kenny, 35, and vice president of an investment company, had many arguments before finding a system that works for them. "With our jobs and no kids, we go out a lot at night," says Sharon. "Sometimes we'd make a double set of plans and forget to tell each other. Then we'd argue over who made the plans first, which plans were more important and who should cancel.

Finally we came up with a solution. We put a monthly calendar on the desk in our bedroom and when we make an appointment, we immediately write it in. We both know to check the calendar before making any dates. That works great for appointments scheduled in advance. When we make last-minute plans and can't check in with each other, we call home and leave a message on our answering machine. It's a lot easier than trying to explain the details to a secretary. We both know to check the messages on our machine by five o'clock to see what's happening. So far, so good—no double plans, no conflicts, no fights."

Whether it's a daily phone call at 4 p.m., morning notes left on each other's pillow or an answering machine check-in, good team communication is imperative for time management.

SAVE TIME AT THE OFFICE

"Make every minute count" has become the motto of many Three-Career Couples. Time-saving tips make the rounds like the latest ethnic joke. As important as they are, however, they should not dwarf our appreciation of what we're saving the time for. Joan Harris, president of a marketing agency in New York, tells of a recent business meeting. While listening to her client, she couldn't help admiring the most magnificent view of the New York skyline she'd seen in years. "Are you too blasé to realize how incredible this view is?" she asked. "Don't you ever swivel around in your chair and look out the window?" When the client admitted that she didn't—ever—Ms. Harris suggested that she look out the window at least once an hour, while taking some long, deep breaths. Time management means not only saving time but savoring it.

Ms. Harris offers these effective time management tips for the office:

■ Use Monday morning—the start of a new week—to plan for the week ahead. Make a master list of what must get done, and, if delegated, write the initials of the person responsible for the task.

■ Keep a tickler file—with folders labeled 1 to 31—for papers that must be retrieved on a specific day of the month. Keep papers in the appropriate folder and check daily for current tasks.

■ Use a handy fax-o-dex, a small rolodex with just fax numbers, to be kept near the fax machine. Life is much easier when you don't have to go scrambling to look up a fax number, especially when you're in a hurry . . . which seems to be most of the time.

■ Keep a file box: a small box near the phone with current files only. It makes for a more efficient office when files can be found immediately.

■ Make appointments for phone calls. Since the game of telephone tag gets very frustrating, setting up specific times for important calls saves everyone time and anxiety. These calls should be treated with as much respect as face-to-face appointments. Put them on your calendar, and prepare for them as you would a meeting.

■ Make business calls right before 5 p.m., to give yourself an excuse to get right to business and the other person a motive for curtailing small talk.

■ Use your lunch hour. A change of environment is healthy and refreshing. Be strict about getting up and out; take some midday time to relax and regroup. If you've got no lunch date, take a magazine to a nearby park or a local luncheonette.

■ Be realistic with time. When making up any kind of work schedule, allow more time than you think you need for each task. Complications like illness, slow mail and interruptions can affect personal productivity. "Haste makes waste" is tired but true.

MAKING YOUR HOME WORK

Your home is your castle, but it seems that most Three-Career Couples are often too busy battling the clock to enjoy their fleeting hours at home. With some organizing, combining of chores and planning ahead you can make life run a little smoother. Even if you don't "beat the clock," you should be able to keep time. Adhering to all the suggestions that follow might be overkill, but adapting one or two bits of advice can help simplify your time at home. It's like setting up a new calendar in January or rewriting your phone book—a pain to anticipate, tedious while you're doing it, but a pleasure to use once it's done.

1) Set up a home headquarters at a desk in the kitchen, your bedroom or the family room.

    • Hang a bulletin board on the wall over the desk for information you want visible: emergency and most-often-used phone numbers, repair list, grocery list, important reminders, etc.

- Put up a monthly calendar for appointments, birthdays, parties, meetings, lessons and activities for the children. Encourage family members to add their appointments, ball games, afterschool activities and meetings.

- To avoid confusion, invest in a pack of colored markers or pencils. Assign each family member a separate color to more easily keep track of who has what on a given day.

- Keep a supply of "home headquarters" necessities: ruler, stamps, stapler, scissors, paper, envelopes, pens, pencils, markers, tape, rubber bands, paper clips, tape measure, hand calculator.

- Keep separate folders for different family members, color coded with the same colors as the calendar. In the folders, keep party invitations, tickets to concerts, reminders. File doctor appointments, car service appointments, teacher conferences, school pictures, etc.

- In a separate folder keep accessible equipment manuals and warranties, home ownership or rental papers, charge receipts, unpaid bills, receipts for paid bills, vacation ideas, gift ideas, gift certificates, correspondence, coupons, miscellaneous information.[4]

2) Use a telephone answering machine. When pressed for time, screen calls and return them at your convenience.

3) Invest in a cordless phone. It allows you to move around while you're talking.

4) Use a VCR. Tape your favorite shows and watch them at your convenience.

5) If you wake up some nights because your mind is working overtime, keep paper and pen by the bed to jot down

those brilliant thoughts that come at 3 a.m. Once you have them on paper, you're less likely to suffer from insomnia.

6) Choose activities that need to be done monthly—like cleaning out the refrigerator or the pantry closet—and pick a time to work as a family team to get them done.

7) Attach a timer to your coffeepot. This saves time in the morning. When you're ready, your coffee will be, too.

AVOID PUTTING THINGS OFF

Just as anticipation can be the best part of a happy event, pro-crastination can be the worst part of an unpleasant task. "To me, one of the worst feelings is the dread that keeps mounting when there's a job I hate to do that I keep putting off, fooling myself that I'm too busy to do it," says Isabel, 35, a paralegal going to law school at night. "Usually I'm pretty responsible about doing what I have to do, but when it comes to changing the clothes in the closets each season or getting my license renewed at motor vehicle or buying a birthday present for my mother-in-law, the job doesn't get done until I take a few aspirins. My husband has his own list of hated chores. He cancels his doctor and dentist appointments three times before he finally gets there, and he's one of those people who mails his tax returns at the post office at 11:00 p.m. on April 15. We're both fine once we start doing the job—we just can't discipline ourselves to begin before we work up a sweat about it."

Putting things off that you want or need to do, choosing some pleasant activity over a more onerous one that is less pleasant but ultimately, when completed, more satisfying, is a familiar but recurrent bad habit of human beings. Postponing unavoid-able tasks and responsibilities just leads to an ever-increasing discomfort level.

We put off working when we:

- are perfectionists and make any task aversive by insisting that it be done 100 percent right;
- take on too many inappropriate commitments and honor those made to another person before those made to ourselves;
- deceive ourselves into thinking we're "preparing" to do the task by relaxing first or reading related material to protect ourselves from feeling guilty; or
- become overwhelmed by the enormity of the task instead of seeing it as a series of small, specific components that are definitely doable.

Whether we procrastinate because we're afraid of failure, success, a person or a situation, whether we dislike the work, are totally bored by it or just plain afraid we're not up to completing it, this is definitely a problem that has clear solutions. In a life as busy as ours, we can't afford the burden of walking around waiting for the ax to drop.

Try implementing one or more of these suggestions (the more abhorrent the job, the more hints you might have to try) the next time you're tempted to trade today for tomorrow:

1) Give yourself a deadline. Say it out loud to those around you, especially to someone who never lets you get away with anything. Write it in big letters on your calendar and in your appointment book.

2) Have everything you need to do the project in one place. If you're paying bills, have stamps, your checkbook, envelopes and pens handy. Make gathering supplies the first part of the task so that you ease into it gradually.

3) Make note of how long it takes to do the dreaded task. Chances are you'll be pleasantly surprised and less apprehensive the next time.

4) Break the job into small, manageable parts. No one wants to clean the basement, but attacking the job in segments (throw away the garbage, rearrange the clutter, dust and vacuum) makes it a tad less awful.

5) Before you begin, make sure there isn't an easier way to get the job done. (If you're planning a trip, for instance, can the travel agent help more with getting the passports, planning an itinerary, getting a taxi to the airport?)

6) Close your eyes and imagine the result and satisfaction of completing the project against the disappointment of a job done late or poorly.

7) Identify potential obstacles before you begin, and decide how to work with them or around them rather than using them as an excuse for delaying work on the project.

8) If the project's a big one, give yourself little rewards as you complete its steps and larger ones once you've finished the entire thing. Think of how good you'll feel once you've got it all done.

9) And lastly, try to figure out why you are procrastinating. If the task isn't important to you or to someone who is important to you, or to your livelihood, then take it out of the list of have-to's in your mind and end the misery.

GIVE UNTO OTHERS TASKS THAT LIFE HAS PILED ONTO YOU

Okay, what happens when there are 24 hours in a day and you need 30 hours to get everything done? Even if you eliminate showering, eating and snuggling with the kids, you still feel like you can't catch up. If you used every timesaving strategy of this chapter, maybe you'd squeeze an extra hour out of your day. It's not enough. It's time to acknowledge that you can't possibly do everything yourself. Delegation is a *must.* Whether it's driving a car pool, dusting and vacuuming your house, doing the background research for a big project or planning and cooking for a dinner party, there are some tasks that can, and should, be hired or "favored" out. Hiring competent help illustrates the truth of cliches like, "You get what you pay for," "It's money well spent," and "Time is money."

"Entrust" is the key word here. Only if you have confidence in someone and you give that person sufficient authority will delegating work. We're assuming here that these are not responsibilities to be shared with partners and children. We'll get to them in Chapter 4. The most frequent reasons people give for not delegating tasks at work and at home are:

- I could do it better than somebody else.
- I have anxiety about someone making mistakes.
- I'm just not comfortable delegating.
- There's no one in whom I feel confident.
- I'm afraid to lose control of the situation.
- I can't afford the cost of hiring someone to help.
- It would take so long to explain to someone how to do it that I might as well just do it myself.[5]

When you stop resisting and realize the benefits of delegating, you will discover an important time management strategy. Once you've chosen the right people for the right job, be patient and give them time to learn. Establish clear guidelines, and assign work gradually and in advance. Don't expect someone to assume total responsibility overnight. Avoid perfectionism. Remember that if someone does it differently, it doesn't mean that it's inferior. Other ways can be just as good as your own.

"It wasn't easy," confesses Jerry, vice president in charge of sales for an importing company. "For ten years the salesmen have always reported to me, and I never thought they would be comfortable working with anyone else. Each salesman calls in once or twice a day, and there are eight of them. Add to that everything else I had to do during the day and I felt like a dog chasing its tail. But I didn't know how to get around it. Then I was out for a few days with the flu. When the salesmen called in, they had to report to my assistant. Lo and behold, he was knowledgeable and efficient and followed up on matters of concern. He was actually more patient and more thorough than I was! At first my ego was a little bruised when I realized that I could so easily be replaced. Then I worried about his competence. Could he handle the ins and outs that had taken me so many years to learn? As he continued to prove himself (and I realized that yes, he still needed me), I started to lighten up and enjoy the relief of one less responsibility. It feels great not to be running in circles anymore!"

SUMMING IT UP

*I'm working so hard on my time management
that I don't get anything else done.*
—Anonymous

It takes time to save time. The initial investment it takes to develop time management skills is necessary, however, in order to enjoy what we promise will be a more efficient scheduling of activities and a smoother-running life.

As a "new" Three-Career Couple, you will fly at the same speed as time if you:

- Recognize that coping styles vary, and there is not just one right way to manage time. It's a waste trying to convert another person's inner rhythms to mirror your own.

- Discover your own best coping style and develop a personal plan for time management. Somewhere in the myriad lists in this chapter is information useful in helping convert unique you into a more efficient unique you.

■ Use a daily, well-planned "To Do" list to stay organized. It's easier to face the day when you know what the day looks like.

■ Manage time both individually and as a team. When the goal is more time for pleasure, what sense does it make not to cooperate?

■ Learn to enjoy the triumph of putting an end to procrastination.

■ Reintroduce the concept of spare time into your life.

■ Delegate the overload to others. You're good, but not so wonderful that no one else around can do as good a job as you.

BUT IT WAS *YOUR* TURN TO EMPTY THE GARBAGE!
Dividing Housework

It is probably not love that makes the world go around, but rather those mutually supportive alliances through which partners recognize their dependence on each other for the achievement of shared and private goals.

Fred Allen, Chairman of Pitney Bowes

There must be more bald eagles left in the world than there are housewives who darn socks, make stew, wash walls and take pride in seeing their face in the kitchen floor. This mythic paragon of love and selfless devotion spent her days at the service of others, nurturing, ego building and ironing shirts. In a lost world of clearly defined gender roles, she was at home when the washing machine repairman came, she was at home at

3 p.m. to greet the school bus and she was at home at 6 p.m. to greet her hero, the provider of the family's resources and the consumer of much of her day's labor. But those are bygone days, and if the current rate of attrition continues, she'll be extinct by the year 2008.[1]

The sons and daughters she lovingly raised with the confidence to do what they want when they want to, are finding it tough to live without her. They find the housework she did all day deadly. It is repetitive and dull and there are no raises or prizes or recognition for a job well done. It's unpaid work without any vacations, sick leave or pension plans. But as inevitable as death and taxes is the fact that somebody's got to be in charge of seeing that there's clean underwear. And who that is, along with who fixes the dinner and who walks the dog, is the bottom line indicator of shared responsibility in three-career families.

The inequitable divvying up of the burden of housework is a central factor in much of current marital discontent. A study of 1,360 married couples by Joan Huber and Glenn Spitze, two sociologists from the University of Illinois, found that how much each spouse earned had no effect on thoughts of divorce. Neither did attitudes about gender roles. What was significant was the amount of housework a wife saw her husband doing. The more he shared, the less likely she was to think of divorce.[2] Women are uncomfortable asking for the help they need because they grew up believing that they should be able to handle everything. Throughout history women have "married up," choosing men more educated and professionally accomplished than themselves (when was the last time you heard of a female doctor marrying a male nurse?). They've tended to see their husband's work as more important than their own and are cautious about demanding too much.

Most men, out there with no role models to guide them, are awkward about learning new behaviors in what they perceive as the woman's domain. They excel at token gestures that stand in psychologically for accepting a full share of responsibility. So they "help out" by barbecuing the hamburgers (not cleaning the grill) or making the salad (not the dressing) or getting the plates into the sink (not the dishwasher) and think they've contributed a fair share to the dinnertime chores.

Arlie Hochschild, in her seminal work, *The Second Shift*, found housework to be shared equally in only one out of five marriages. Men, on average, contributed one third of the work, and one in ten did less. When men do their share, it's performing nondaily tasks like repairing appliances, mowing the lawn or taking care of the car. Women are always on duty; men control how and when they will help.[3]

Things are no better in other countries either. A 1992 report issued by the International Labor Organization, a United Nations agency, said that worldwide, women have primary—and oftentimes sole—responsibility for the care of their family and their home. There might be much to envy about Japan's work ethic, but it does not extend to the husband's role at home. Men there spend only 15 minutes a day on household chores. In Cuba there's actually a law requiring men to do their fair share around the house, but, as you can imagine, enforcement is a low priority. It's hard to picture the police knocking on the door and saying, "Okay buster, turn off that TV and get out of that recliner. That's your second baseball game today. Get on all fours and scrub that kitchen floor!" And in the Scandinavian countries where the work week has been shortened, any spare hours husbands have are spent on leisure activities, not on work at home.[4]

Research tells us that no matter how many hours a week a woman works outside the home, she still does significantly more housework than her man, says Gayle Rawlings, a counselor at Briarcliffe College in Hicksville, New York. Men perceive that they do a lot more than they actually do, which usually amounts to helping the woman who is orchestrating the master plan and delegating jobs that she can't handle on her own.

Since it is women who manage the Third Career, they must adjust their expectations at home during the workweek—learn to ignore the dust on the coffee table and the pile of dirty clothes on the laundry room floor—and develop a tolerance for the unavoidable weekday chaos found in most three-career homes.

According to Ms. Rawlings, while sexism still prevails in the usual division of chores, this pattern doesn't always work. And when it doesn't, couples must talk about what they like and don't like to do around the house. If he hates the vacuuming and she hates the laundry, a workable arrangement can be made.

"I always hated sorting and folding laundry," admits Audrey, a 32-year-old bookkeeper. "But it was one of those jobs that had to be done. I never even thought about discussing it with Greg; what was the point? Then one night we were having dinner with friends and somehow the subject of housework came up. When I mentioned how I dreaded that monstrous pile of laundry staring me down at the end of a long day, Greg was truly surprised."

"I never knew Audrey looked at it that way," Greg adds. "Usually after dinner we all sit on our bed to watch the news. While Audrey folded the laundry I always went through the mail—and got worked up and tense looking at all the bills. I would much rather fold towels and T-shirts, believe me. But neither of us ever thought of suggesting a switch. It's amazing how well it's turned out; I just wish Audrey had told me sooner."

HONEY, WHERE DO YOU KEEP THE ICE CUBES?

Most women, even if they're not close to living up to their

mother's standards, regard the home as their turf and expect acknowledgment as the household "maven." Unfortunately you can't have it both ways, playing both the expert and super-woman in spurts and then feel angry when curt requests for help are not immediately acknowledged or properly handled. Nobody knows that better than Jane and Bernie, whose gourmet dinner turned to disaster on the evening that Bernie's mom came to visit.

"It was a case of unfair expectations," according to Bernie. "One of those 'magic' moments in every marriage when suddenly your best intentions backfire and you feel dumber than dumb! It started out as such a nice evening. We both had great days at work, and the baby was in a particularly playful mood. My mother just came up from Florida, and Jane and I were happy to see her. We saw how our competence allayed her fears that with both of us working, the baby, the house and our relationship would suffer. Jane fixed a great-looking salad and even had time to try out a new sauce to go with the pasta. When we eat at home, she shops and cooks, I clean up—that's our deal.

"When I got home from work my mother and Jane were sitting in the kitchen, waiting for the pasta to finish boiling and catching up on the past few months. I asked if there was anything I could do to help, and Jane said that if I would just get the pasta to the table—the sauce was in the pot next to it—then she could finish giving the baby his bottle. Now she knows that I never made pasta before. Looking back, of course, I should've said something. But it didn't seem as if it would be that complicated. And how do you say in front of your mother that you're an MBA who doesn't know how to get pasta from the pot to the table?

"I stuck a teaspoon in the sauce and previewed a sample. Then with a flourish I gave it a final stir and poured the pot of sauce into the pot of boiling pasta. While I was still pouring I realized that something wasn't right, but it wasn't until I heard

Jane's scream that it hit me what I had done. Jane's rich, thick red sauce, now diluted in three quarts of water, was thin and soupy with pieces of tomato and herbs floating on the top.

"Okay, I admit, I screwed up. I forgot to drain the water. And the colander was right there in the sink, waiting. It was a dumb mistake. I wish I could say that I just wasn't concentrating, but, the truth is, I didn't know what to do and was too embarrassed to ask. However, I didn't kill anybody. And I certainly didn't do it intentionally. Jane came down on me like I was the biggest idiot ever to live. It'll be a long time before I'll offer to help her out in the kitchen again."

Jane's perspective of the situation naturally was quite different. "It was beyond my comprehension that a 39-year-old man who had lived on his own for ten years, runs a successful business, and is a husband and father and the man I chose to spend the rest of my life with, would not know that you have to drain the water from the pot before you pour the sauce on the pasta. It's true, I lost my temper and said some pretty cruel things. And I probably shouldn't have embarrassed him in front of his mother—although I think she probably agreed with me—but I was so tired and it was such a small thing to ask. I guess I took it for granted that everyone knows how to do such a simple thing. Next time I'll keep that in mind when I ask him to help out with my half of the chores."

WHEN IT COMES TO VACUUMING, ANATOMY STILL DETERMINES DESTINY

In the future, men are going to have to overcome their ignorance and work around the economic and cultural excuses they use for not doing their fair share. But again, that's the future. In the present tense many see getting involved with "women's work" as a loss of power. Their fathers came home, kissed their kids' foreheads and sat down and read the paper. Bosses don't set tables or throw in a load of wash when they walk in from a hard day. Some believe a greater earning capacity and their frequent long and inflexible hours earn them more leisure time. Some react as if energy were a measurable quantity and if they expend too much at home, they'll produce less at work. And others complain that their wives' high standards of cleanliness and tidiness ("Why do we need a butter dish on the table? You can't even see what's on the top shelf, why does it have to be dusted every week?) are totally unreasonable.

The National Longitudinal Surveys of Labor Market Experience begun in the late 60s by the U.S. Department of Labor followed groups of 5,000 young men and women from adolescence through adulthood and 5,000 older men and women over a period of 15 years. The results, as reported by Linda Waite and Frances Goldscheider in *New Families, No Families? The Transformation of the American Home* are not what you might expect:

- Married men with more education share significantly more in every chore—except for yard and household maintenance (which they hire others to take care of)—than do married men with less education.

- Married men with postgraduate degrees take 30 to 50 percent more responsibility than do married men with eighth-grade educations for dishwashing, child care, shopping, housecleaning and laundry.

- When both have postgraduate educations, husbands do 80 percent more housework than do husbands in homes where both have eighth-grade educations.

- The presence of children generally reduces a husband's domestic participation, especially if there are teenage daughters living at home. A husband's help is greatest before children arrive and after they depart.

Wives will also have an easier time soliciting help from husbands raised in homes with a single mother. They've grown up with increased responsibilities and expect to do their share. (Interestingly, when wives come from female-headed households, they are more accustomed than traditional women to having household work done by women and children, and they tend to do a greater portion of such work themselves.)[5]

The fact that men and women are marrying later also works toward a more equitable distribution of housework. Men who've lived on their own for a while are more familiar with the operation of a household. Their experience makes it more difficult for them to sleep guiltfree and ignore the fact that women put in an extra month of 24-hour days a year doing housework than do their husbands—that breaks down to 22.6 hours a week of housework and child care versus a husband's average of 7.4 hours a week.[6]

HOW DO I KNOW IF YOU DON'T TELL ME?

Effective communication between partners has always been the cornerstone of successful relationships, but for today's Three-Career Couple it is more important than ever to be sensitive to each other's feelings, says Adele Faber, co-author with Elaine Mazlish of *How to Talk So Kids Will Listen and Listen So Kids Will Talk*. Whether dividing up housework or making other decisions, the problem-solving approach can be especially helpful.

- What do you need?
- What do I need?
- Let's brainstorm for possible solutions.
- Let's decide on the best solution.

But what if the "best" solution doesn't work? Together, ask:

- Are we hearing each other?
- Is the arrangement we've developed working? or,

- Are we adhering to rigid rules that seemed right one month ago but aren't working now?
- Is either of us resentful or angry over a specific arrangement? and finally,
- If something isn't working, what can we change to make it work better?

If you don't regularly renegotiate the way you've divided household chores, how will you know if one partner is feeling an undue burden or needs more support? Naturally, there will be those thankless tasks that neither partner wants to do. Who wouldn't rather avoid scrubbing the ring in the bathtub? Can anyone find any redeeming value in emptying the dishwasher? But if tackled with a team spirit, the whole issue takes on a different feeling.

"Attitude is the key," says Ms. Faber. "Partners should approach the division of labor with a spirit of, 'Okay, let's divide up the chores so we can have time left over to enjoy each other.' One partner might say, 'Well, I like fresh air at night, so I'll take out the garbage.' The other might continue with, 'Okay, I guess I'll do the vacuuming; it's good exercise.' You can laugh, you can trade, and remember that no arrangement need be permanent. If it turns out a month later that it's not working, reassess the situation. Are there any changes we can make? Should we trade jobs. . . do them together. . . do them differently? The key is a willingness to experiment and be creative."

Sometimes "creative" teamwork can mean an unexpected trip to the department store to buy pots and pans! "We've both always hated cooking," says Carole (the school superintendent we met in Chapter 1). "We always had a nice neat kitchen filled with paper plates in different colors and an empty cabinet where the pots and pans are supposed to go. It was never important to Joe or me; as long as we served our children healthy, nutritious meals, we agreed we were doing fine. So we never argued over who would cook; the big decision every night was who would bring home the deli sandwiches or pick up the Chinese food."

Only once, Carole remembers, their domestic arrangement created a dilemma. "Since Joe worked closer to home than I did, he always volunteered to be the 'class mother' in our children's school. One November afternoon our son came home with a request for his dad to come up to school to help the children cook a Thanksgiving dinner. He had a list of items to bring: the potatoes and onions just meant a quick trip to the grocery, but the two cooking pots were the problem! That night after dinner we ran out and bought our first set of pots and pans so that the "class mother" could save face the next day. My son still insists that his dad's turkey stew was the best (and probably the only!) he ever had."

The Dirt on Men

A 1990 survey of 5,000 married couples done by the Conference Board, a nonprofit research organization, revealed:

- 86% of husbands rarely or never iron
- 62% of husbands rarely or never do laundry
- 50% of husbands refuse to take out the garbage[7]

It's the extra, almost invisible chores crammed into a day that drive many women over the edge. They're the kind that don't take much time, but even a few minutes are stressful when you don't have a moment to spare. The most helpful man in the world is unlikely to send out birthday cards, write letters to extended family, water the plants, shop for children's clothes, pick out presents, sew on a button, make the bed, feed the cat or bring an appliance in to be repaired. You can't blame men for not realizing the extra burden these tasks entail; most of them seem to just get accomplished magically.

Take Karen and Steve, for example. For too long Karen, 35 and a writer, kept her feelings of being overwhelmed and taken for granted to herself. "I never knew how to explain to Steve what it was like to work from home. What it was like trying to sound professional doing a phone interview with a professor from Harvard while five four-year-olds were killing each other in the background; or trying to live through a mile-wide writer's block because tomorrow is the deadline for a 10,000-word magazine article, while being expected to get to the shoemaker, argue with the insurance company and help out with the homework—before starting dinner. So many times I've wished I could escape and empty my mind of everything but my work, like Steve does every morning. But then I see the exhaustion all over his face when he comes home, stressed out after his long day, and I feel guilty asking him to stop and pick up a few groceries on the way home. So I grit my teeth, add one more stop to my afternoon and try not to resent it."

Steve eventually learned, without Karen having to tell him, what a day in her life was like. "I couldn't have planned it better if I tried," Karen laughs. "It was a typical day, no better or worse than any other, but what he witnessed brought home loud and clear what I wanted him to know."

"I really thought we both had everything under control," he remembers. "I admit that because Karen works at home all day I diminished the importance of what she does. I just took for granted that she could juggle all the parts of her life with no problem. Her assignments were always in on time; the children never seemed to suffer. And she was initially so grateful to have a job where she could be around for the kids that I thought she really had the best of both worlds. There was no reason for me to believe she couldn't do her interviewing and writing and still fit in the laundry and the car pools and whatever else she had to do around the house.

"Then I threw my back out and had to stay home from work for three days. I wasn't in any real pain as long as I followed the doctor's prescription for bed rest. I expected that nothing would be more important to Karen than making time for me—that she'd stop whatever it was she usually does and give me a little TLC. Boy, did I have that wrong!

"From 8 until 5, the woman never stopped. I think she was working on three different projects, and I heard her on the phone all morning. When she came into the bedroom I thought it was to check on me, but instead she dumped two baskets of laundry on the bed and started to sort while cradling the phone on her shoulder, recording a conversation with a new phone attachment she just bought to leave her hands free for folding the wash.

"At lunchtime, when Karen left for an hour—to bring home Lisa and a friend from nursery school, stop to pick up stuff for dinner and get my suit from the cleaners—the phone rang four times. When she got home she started tracking down the people she missed during her "break." Karen interrupted what she was doing three more times that day—to take Jason to the orthodontist, to give instructions to the guy who cuts the grass and to drive Jason and three friends to soccer practice.

"Now I understand why she falls asleep every night by ten o'clock. It's amazing how I underestimated how much she accomplishes in one day. I'm going to really try to be more aware of her work load and help out a little more at home."

STRATEGIC HELPLESSNESS

It's a commonly held belief that men take a role in domestic labor only if *they* want to. And even though they are wanting to in greater numbers each year, it's still one of those good news/ bad news deals. Fifty-eight percent of husbands advocate equal division of labor while only 33 percent assume a significant portion of family chores.[8] Interestingly, there seems to be a ris-

What Men Will—and Won't—Do
Tasks men find acceptable (based on no scientific study):

- raking leaves
- cleaning drain pipes
- putting up storm windows
- walking the dog
- barbecuing
- maintaining the car
- making home repairs
- filing tax returns
- organizing the garage
- changing light bulbs/batteries

Tasks they probably will never do (based on no scientific study):

- pair socks ("I swear, I can't tell the difference")
- wrap a gift ("What birthday?")
- wash anything in hot-enough water ("Wear gloves—are you *kidding?*")
- dust ("I don't see it")
- use elbow grease to scour or scrub anything inside the house ("Nothing's that important—or that dirty")
- polish silver ("too wimpy")
- clean the tile in the bathroom ("Only if you're nine months' pregnant")
- throw away the last smidgen of ice cream in the container ("why?")

ing standard of male consideration that's independent of the number of hours their wives spend working outside the home. A Boston University job and home life study revealed "no significant difference between married males with employed wives and those with nonemployed wives on the number of hours per week the husband spends on home chores."[9] Some women have found using feminine wiles a way around those husbands who work on their car or bring in firewood and are ready to call it a day. We call it "strategic helplessness."

Men have difficulty taking orders and accepting criticism from their wives concerning the way they perform home chores. It's in their genes, just like the way they refuse to ask for directions and have trouble staying awake at subtitled foreign films. But there's nothing they do better than rescuing the woman they love from a situation she can't seem to handle. There are millions of men who take care of paying bills because their wives convinced them they "can't" do it. Women who carefully calculate their incompetence get cooperation from chivalrous husbands who would never ordinarily pick up that extra part for the vacuum—"Honey, I know I'll get lost if I try to find that place"— or negotiate price with the air conditioner repairman—"He'll never listen to me." Husbands who should know better can't resist being a hero. A woman's capacity for feeling grateful (and expressing it) gets her more help around the house than any legal agreement ever could.

"I made up my mind never to learn how to fix the timer on the outside lights or program the VCR," Karen says forcefully. "The more I know, the more I'm expected to do. I figured out how to use our camcorder, and now it's my job to take all the pictures on holidays and special occasions. The day I learned how to use the snowblower was the last day Steve ever cleared the driveway. I swore ignorance is bliss, and now I just play dumb. But I'm aware that two can play the game. He'll spend ten minutes trying to make the bed without lumps. He acts like

I'm a genius for making such delicious Rice Krispies treats when he knows all you do is mix four things together in a bowl. And even though I know better, he'd bet money that it's beyond his intelligence to sew on a button, use a word processor or carve a pumpkin. Meanwhile, he loves remembering to set the timer to tape *Seinfeld* so I won't miss it when I'm at a press club dinner. And I love seeing his grateful face after I magically get a stain out of his favorite shirt. Being appreciated makes all the difference in the world."

"Knowing that you don't have to learn how to do everything, that you can trust someone else to fill in the blanks, is one of the best things about being married. I know sometimes we're each playing a game, but so far for us we're both winning."

SOME SUCCESS STORIES

It might take another generation or two before the word "marriage" is entirely free of its connotation as a historic exchange of female services for male incomes. Even for couples with the best of intentions, the concept of sharing rather than helping when it comes to husbands and housework is difficult to implement.

"Art and I did a lot of talking about this issue before we got married," says Leslie, 38, a dentist and mother of a nine-year-old daughter. "The way our parents lived was not the way we envisioned our lives. As soon as Lara was born we each painstakingly rearranged our schedules. We agreed to work on alternating days—three and a half days each, 12 hours a day. That left one of us always home to care for her. The at-home parent that day makes the rules, shops, cleans, does laundry—whatever has to be done. Now that our daughter's older, neither one of us is chomping at the bit to go back to work full time. There's a financial price to pay, but it's worth it for us."

"It was difficult at first," continues Art, 37, a psychologist. "When I'd be home watching *Sesame Street* at 9:30 on a Tuesday morning and all my friends were busy 'making it' buying new cars and bigger homes, I had my moments of doubt. When I sat down on a bench near the playground, I felt like a woman might at an all-night poker game. It took Leslie a while to get over feeling she was relinquishing control at home. She tried to get me to diaper Lara the same way she did (the right way, she was sure) until she noticed a woman in her play group diapering the same way I was. It was an epiphany for her—acknowledging that different was simply different, not better or worse. That lesson has kept us both honest throughout the years. The best part of this arrangement is that we both understand that the grass is the same shade of green (or brown) on both sides of the fence. And we both agree that the day we go to the office is the easier day."

"Getting Bob to be more comfortable sharing domestic chores was easier once I gave up trying to assign him the jobs I wanted him to do," says Susan a 40-year old publicist. "He was great at playing dumb ('Does this light blue shirt get washed in hot or cold water?' 'What does this water-saver thing mean on the dishwasher?' 'Do I wrap these leftovers in plastic wrap or foil or plastic bags or freezer wrap?'), and I invariably lost patience and did the chore myself.

"It took years until I realized I could have his full cooperation if I worked toward his interests and strengths. So now while he hates shopping in the supermarket, he has no problem finding a place for everything in the refrigerator and the pantry when I unpack. He would never pick up an iron, but he loves the new steamer I bought. (It's sleek, black and expensive—right up his alley.) And this year for Father's Day the girls bought him a Dirt Devil. He has never vacuumed in his life, but now that he owns this red, powerful, shiny piece of machinery (advertised as having the power of an upright in the palm of the hand), he willingly cleans up small spills and messes. If I could only find some more household tools made of Goretex and mesh, maybe with a Harley-Davidson logo, I'd have this sharing thing solved!"

"Because Kenny is in the dry-cleaning business, and his days are very long. When he's home, he wants to spend time with the boys," say Karen, 33, an advertising representative for a community newspaper and the mother of two sons, seven and three. "I agreed that bonding time was a priority, but I needed his help as well. Now we kill two birds with one stone. On Sunday morning at ten o'clock, my three males leave the house with a list. They do the supermarket shopping, return library books, buy sneakers and hit Home Depot before coming home. In those few hours I'm able to throw in a few loads of laundry and make (and freeze) dinner for three nights during the week. Then we reunite about two o'clock and spend the rest of Sunday together. As long as I know I can count on four hours of Kenny's help to do errands and take care of the kids, I can manage the rest."

WHY INVOLVE THE KIDS?

Involving children in housework instills a valuable sense of responsibility, insist some child experts. Fostering children's participation in family chores builds character, add others. How about involving the kids because we just plain don't have the time—or energy—to do everything ourselves? How often do you hear, "I have no time!" when you ask your children to set the table/empty the dishwasher/walk the dog? What about the "But I have to do my homework!" or "I'm studying for a spelling test!" responses? Do our children really think we are oblivious to the hours they spend in front of the TV, on the phone or playing computer games? Since they share in eating the family dinner every night, why shouldn't they share in its preparation and cleanup as well? They contribute generously to the hamper full of dirty clothes; isn't it logical they should also share in emptying that hamper into the washing machine or in folding the clean laundry? Somehow we have to reintroduce logic into our reality.

But bringing logic back into reality may be a long road to travel, especially for those Three-Career Couples who minimize their children's roles in household responsibilities. In fact, based on the studies reported by Frances Goldscheider and Linda Waite in *New Families, No Families?*:

- There is little evidence that mothers' employment has much, if any, effect on the extent to which children share in household tasks. If she works and decreases her involvement in household tasks, so, too, do her children.

- Women who value work-related roles for women share responsibility less with their children—particularly cooking and laundry—than do women in traditional families with stay-at-home mothers.

- Maternal education influences the participation of children in household chores. Children's share decreases with increases in the number of years of school the mother has completed. For every four additional years of education the mother has attained, children share about a third of a chore less.

Authors Goldscheider and Waite conclude that "highly educated mothers evidently prefer that their children spend time studying algebra or writing their English compositions rather than on household chores." At the same time, there is a tendency among more-educated mothers to share less responsibility with their daughters and more with their sons—seemingly wanting to prepare their sons for domestic independence.

Getting kids to pitch in begins with the same basic principle that applies to Three-Career Couples: a spirit of cooperation. According to author Adele Faber, too often families operate on threats and punishment. "This is pure poison," she says. "It creates hostility and resentment, erodes self-esteem and is self-defeating. If you involve the children in the problem-solving process, you have a much better chance of getting them to cooperate. This is not a gimmick; it's a lifestyle that can be started early, when children are small."

The problem-solving approach for families, just as for couples, relies on listening to each other's feelings, brainstorming for solutions, agreeing on the solutions and then reevaluating them with an openness to change if they're not working.

Given that there is a house full of chores that need to be done, two working parents and children at home, what should children be expected to do? According to Toni Liebman, an early childhood specialist, it's important for parents to know what is realistic at different ages and to set appropriate expectations accordingly. Preschool children can be encouraged to participate in simple household chores, while older children can be expected to do so on a regular basis. At any age children gain a sense of accomplishment and satisfaction from being part of the "family team." Chores should be assigned by preference, convenience and ability—not by gender.

According to Goldscheider and Waite, the home is still a gender factory. Girls tend to spend twice as much time on housework as their brothers, mirroring the different levels of contribution by their mothers and fathers. Families with teenage girls report sharing five times more household tasks with children than do families with boys of the same age. Of all children, girls between the ages of 12 and 18 seem to carry the largest share of housework, while boys contribute little and participate mainly in yard work. "While parents want their daughters to marry liberated men who will share in the housework so that these daughters can be successful, they are preparing their *sons* to marry traditional women who will carry the household burden themselves to further their son's career."

HOW DO YOU DIVVY UP THE CHORES?

Like almost every issue addressed in this book, there is not just one right way to tackle the challenge. What works for one family may be ineffective for another.

For Ron (the ex-bowler we met in Chapter 2), Barbara and their three preteen children, a Sunday afternoon family meeting is used to assign chores for the week. "At our first meeting we made a list of all the jobs that needed to be done around the house," explains Barbara. "The list included everything from cleaning the house to taking care of the dog, cat, fish and birds to going shopping and doing laundry and dinnertime activities. There are some jobs that were automatically assigned to an adult, just based on practicality. The kids can't drive, so obviously they couldn't do the food shopping. The rest of the chores get divided up by choice—or in some cases, by reason of who hates each the least. Tommy takes the animals every week because his sisters hate them and they live in his room. Melissa usually sets the table because she likes coming up with new ways to fold the napkins. For the most part assignment is voluntary, and by now we have it pretty much down to a science. If one week no one will take a specific job—like the bathrooms— we try to rotate or come up with some ingenious way to assign it. Last week Melissa agreed to do the bathrooms if she could pawn off other chores to her brother and sister. They agreed and split the rest of her jobs—anything not to have to do the bathrooms."

Susan (the teacher introduced in Chapter 2) and Arthur (her husband who can't lie still in his hammock) also tried family meetings, but they were a disaster. "No one could agree," admits Susan. "These meetings turned into screaming matches, with Melanie always crying that she got the worst deal. In desperation I came up with another idea. Out of cardboard I made a wheel with ten different chores we agreed would be done by the kids. There was nothing terrible on it, just jobs like folding the laundry, watering the plants and emptying the dishwasher. Then I made a spinner out of a piece of paper and a paper fastener, and now, once a week, the girls take turns spinning the wheel until the ten chores are divided. They feel like it's a game, and it takes some of the pain out of pitching in around the house."

The power of games should never be underestimated with children. Try turning a boring activity into a game—"Let's race to see who gets his or her room cleaned first!" "First one to finish two chores gets a free favor from Mom and Dad!" "Let's divide up these 12 jobs—one point for each job done. If we get ten points by noon, we'll all go out for ice cream sundaes!" Family meetings become powwows if they're held sitting in a circle on the carpet in the dark, with each member holding a flashlight. A weekly schedule can be posted on the refrigerator or displayed on posterboard with fluorescent markers in a heavily trafficked hallway.

"In our house if it's not on the calendar, it doesn't happen," says Kathy, 45, a police officer and wife of a fellow police officer. "Our plumber gave out this great calendar with two-inch square boxes, so we can fill everything in: our work schedules, the kids' activities and family chores. Everything in our family goes by the month. The calendar has become such a ritual that we never do anything without writing it in. When the kids trade chores, they run right to the calendar. It keeps us organized and on schedule and is a constant reminder of what we each have to do. We've all learned to write in pencil because there are so many changes. My only concern is that I just heard that the plumbing company went out of business. Now I'm on the lookout for another calendar with big enough boxes—or we'll all fall apart!"

With any family plan, the more children are involved in the problem-solving process, the more important they'll feel and the less they'll resent the responsibility. "In my own family," recalls author Adele Faber, "a neglected family pet prompted a problem-solving experience for my children. No one was taking care of the dog. I was forever nagging, reminding, demanding, and nothing was working. I knew we needed a fresh approach. Finally I told the children to go into another room, have a conference with each other and not come out until they had a solution. Fifteen minutes later they emerged with a chart they had drawn with a rotating schedule; my oldest son proudly hung it on the wall. I noticed that my youngest son who was seven at the time, seemed unhappy about the plan. After some questioning I discovered that he was frightened of walking the dog at night. "'It won't work,' I told the children. 'This chart does not take everyone's feelings into consideration. You need to go back to the drawing board'. Their final resolution: the seven-year-old eliminated his night walk and took an extra morning walk instead. The three of them were proud that they came up with the plan on their own—and they stuck to it."

IT DOESN'T ALWAYS COME NATURALLY

When our children complain that they can't vacuum because they don't know how to, when they make their beds with lumps and wrinkles or mix up socks while sorting, it could be the same "strategic helplessness" they see watching their parents in action. Or perhaps they just need some direction and patient instruction. It's not fair to expect a child to know how to do something without ever having learned how, says author Sally Wendkos Olds, author of *The Working Parents' Survival Guide.* "We often assume that our children know how to perform certain tasks because they've seen us do them so many times. But think of your children as being like passengers in a car being driven by someone else. You may travel the route a dozen times, but it's very likely that you won't learn the route until you have to drive it yourself. Unless you're responsible for reaching your destination, you're apt to put your attention on the changing colors of the foliage or the joggers on the road or the clothes in the shop windows, instead of on landmarks and mileage and turns. It's the same with children."[10]

Child experts advise breaking a job down into smaller parts and going through the steps with children—first showing them how to do a job, having them do it with you, then by themselves under your supervision and finally on their own—praising them along the way for a job well done, correcting them tactfully if they fall short and employing your willpower to hold back from redoing the job yourself.[11]

"Sometimes it seems easier to do everything myself," confesses Peggy, the office manager and mother of three we first met in Chapter 2. "The living room coffee table always has fingerprints on it, the dinner table is often set backwards and I can never find my dishes in the cabinets they're supposed to be in. But it's a trade-off for the 45 minutes a day I have to soak in a hot bath and read the newspaper—time I'd never have if I had to do those chores that the children have taken over."

Other Creative Approaches

If parents blame and accuse ("How many times do I have to tell you?"), name call ("Look at the way you did that; it's disgusting!"), threaten ("If you don't finish your chores, you're grounded!") and compare ("Your brother's bed is much neater!"), they are almost guaranteeing a kid will turn them off—not to mention that they're instilling feelings of anger, fear and inadequacy in their children.

"These are things I hate to do so much that they can ruin my week. Can anyone help?" So read a sign that Iris (the nurse in Chapter 2 who no longer feels any guilt) posted by the front door, along with a pen hanging from a string. When she came home from work that evening, she found that most of the chart had been filled in. "A little creativity and a call for help really worked," says Iris. "They really 'got' how much I needed them and asking in this way gave them the opportunity to feel virtuous."

Once you exhaust the resources in your immediate family, don't be afraid to dip into an extended network. Babysitters can cut up vegetables for a salad or set the table while the baby naps; grandparents may enjoy updating a photo album—especially if you promise to make them copies of the latest pictures. Those tasks for which it's impossible to find a helping hand might require hiring someone. College students are often looking to pick up extra cash and may not mind doing your most dreaded chores. And then there's always the subtle approach....

"I was tired of screaming," says June, a 39-year-old sales rep for a beauty supply company. "So I decided the best way to make my point was by doing nothing. Literally. For jobs not done by the kids, the consequences were only logical—when they didn't put their clothes in the hamper, the clothes didn't get washed. When their beds weren't made before school, I closed their doors and didn't touch their rooms—they stayed unvacuumed and undusted. When no one emptied the dishwasher, I served dinner with no plates on the table. I put the garbage pail inside the room of the child assigned to bring it to the curb. It took four days (two longer than I hoped it would), but everyone got the point. They now know I mean business, and although they still grumble, they know that fair is fair."

SUMMING IT UP

Sometimes it's hard for women to understand that the reason they're not getting all the help they need from their spouses is not that men are innately lazier or clumsier or more selfish, but that in matters pertaining to dust and dirt there is a perception gap. Women must admit to contributing to the creating and maintaining of gender imbalances. Their spouses' lack of cooperation comes more from insensitivity and societal expectations than from malice or lack of love.

"Men have a greater tolerance for disorder," explains Bruce, 39, a high school teacher. "Women are more neurotic about dirt.

To them it symbolizes chaos and despair. To us it's just a condition to be ignored . . . until we can't anymore. It's not hostility that makes us leave crumbs on the counter or rinse a glass with cold water, it's just that we don't see those things as important. Intellectually we know that we should clean the toilet bowl once in a while, but images of Dagwood in an apron are stronger than doing what's fair."

It's only human nature to try to get away with as few onerous tasks as we can in this lifetime, so the burden to present a more equitable distribution of household chores as life enhancing falls to women. If women don't push (begging, crying, nagging and withholding sex, the most popular expressions of disapproval, haven't worked in this century), men won't change. Women have to convince their families that the rewards are well worth the effort. Here are some approaches you might find successful.

With your spouse

1) The rational approach—If both of us work together this afternoon to get the house in order, instead of you watching TV and me growling at you as I vacuum under your feet, we'll have tonight to have some fun, with neither of us tired or resentful.

2) The good health approach—Marriage and family therapist John Gottman studied 73 couples over a four-year period and found that men who did housework were far healthier than those who did not. Helpful men were not as overwhelmed by their wives' emotions and had lower heart rates during marital conflict than men who did no housework.[12]

3) The "it's the 90s'" approach—Respecting your wife as an equal, valuing the integrity of her career as you do your own, being reliable, independent and a true partner is today's definition of masculine. Ignorance is . . . igno-

rance. Today's wimp is not the guy cleaning the fish tank
but the one who can't find the ketchup, the one who can't
make anything but cereal for dinner, the one who'll wear
a dirty shirt rather than go to the cleaners. "Macho" as a
concept is going the way of the Bee Gee's, junk bonds
and rotary phones.

4) The "I promise I won't look too closely" approach—
Acknowledge that each partner may have a different
timetable and a different definition of clean. Compromising on what tasks are the most palatable and when a
given chore has to be completed (maybe a week to do a
list posted on the refrigerator?) is crucial. Agreeing not to
remind or prod in between and accepting the results without criticizing can lead to more enthusiastic cooperation
between partners. Either subtly or explicitly, start expecting his help on a regular basis. So what if you can do it
faster and better—if you have to do it alone.

5) The "I will appeal to your sense of justice" approach—
Open your man's eyes to how much you're doing. A
black-and-white accounting of the time each partner
spends on housework has to wake up the most compla-
cent partner. A more equitable settlement can be reached
by assessing how balanced your situation is, renegotiat-
ing changes and dividing tasks according to the amount
of time each partner spends at home.

6) The "boost to intimacy" approach—A more symmetrical
division of labor can't help but enhance a relationship.
Hopefully the development of new domestic skills will
be rewarded with a sense of accomplishment and pleasure. Closeness comes from sharing, and men who feel
like strangers in their own homes ("Where is the
Ajax?"—or worse—"What *is* Ajax?"), who regard participating in the Third Career as a loss to their standard of

living, must hold themselves accountable for a resentment that can prevent true intimacy from occurring.

And with the kids

7) Adapt #1 ("Let's work together and then go to the amusement park!"); #4 ("I promise I won't yell if you overcook the spaghetti or you miss the corners when you vacuum"); #5 ("You're old enough to understand that Mom can't do it all." "I don't care if you're a boy or a girl—you are each capable and competent to clean this brownie pan *and* clean up the dog's mess!")

And finally, #6 ("We're a family; let's be a team!").

AND WE THOUGHT LABOR WAS HARD!
The Biggest Part of the Third Career: Children

You give kids a choice: their mother in the next room on the verge of suicide versus their mother in Hawaii in ecstasy. They'll pick suicide in the next room, believe me.

Nora Ephron

In our culture, to fulfill the job description of a good parent you must forever more delegate your own needs to second place, after satisfying those of your children. As Nora Ephron reminds us, what is good news for mothers careerwise (a promotion, a move, greater responsibility) is invariably bad news for her kids.[1] According to the findings of the National Com-

mission on Children's Survey of Children and Parents, 88 percent of American adults believe it is harder to be a parent today
than it used to be.[2] While most parents are happy with the quality of their relationship with their children, 59 percent wish
they had more time to spend with them.[3] Most of the literature
on the double bind of staying home and providing values, discipline and security over the personal satisfaction and economic
advantages of working outside of the home focuses on mothers.
Yet most children of employed parents are less likely to be satisfied with the amount of time they spend with their fathers than
that which they spend with their mothers.[4]

Parents are not immune to the uncertainty and guilt that
comes along with the package of three careerdom. To lessen
that torn-apart feeling, we are about to raise a generation of
"gourmet babies." In the 1950s, one out of ten families had
only one child; today it's one out of four. In 1965, three children were the norm; today it's 1.89. Four times as many women
today compared to 15 years ago are having their first child
between the ages of 35 and 39.[5] And no matter how many kids
there are in the family, or the age of the parents, parent-child
interactions are decreasing. Regardless of their work situation
outside the home, parents today spend 40 percent less time with
their children than did parents in 1965, according to data col-
lected from personal time diaries by sociologist John Robinson
at the University of Maryland. In 1965, parents spent approximately 30 hours a week with their children. By 1985, it was
down to 17 hours a week.[6]

"I know I spend fewer hours with my kids than my parents
did with me," says Jennifer, a 31-year-old saleswoman and
mother of two, "but I'm not sure that's necessarily bad. Actually, I think my husband had a tougher time adapting to me
being less available when I went back to work than the kids did.
I grew up with a mother who spent hours coaxing us to be good
eaters—the more we ate, the better job she was doing. She did

everything to ensure that I wouldn't have to work too hard. It wasn't until I got married that I learned to sew and iron and cook and do laundry. My mom's motives were 100 percent pure, but her overwhelming input often made me feel that I was incapable of handling anything difficult."

"Our parents might have been home more," continues Ray, Jennifer's 35-year-old husband and a social worker, "but I wouldn't exactly call the time they spent with us 'quality.' They thought obedience, conformity and respect for authority were the most important traits to instill in us. That still didn't keep me from cheating in high school, trying drugs in college or marrying out of my religion. Our kids are being raised with independence, tolerance, hard work and helping others as their building blocks. Just like learning how to use a calculator has replaced the study of long division in elementary school, we've cut down on rigid household rules in favor of a looser, more democratic and self-reliant exchange of ideas. Maybe I'm rationalizing, but I honestly think my kids will grow up stronger and more capable than I did."

"I think being the mother you believe your kids deserve is impossible, whether you're at home or working full-time," says Bonnie, a 29-year-old mother of three who works as a data processor. "I've given up baking cookies and making Halloween costumes because there's no time, but even if there were, I'd still fall short of the patient, even-tempered, always-available miracle worker I somehow thought I would be."

Unfortunately some parents, in an attempt to alleviate their discomfort with the amount of time they physically spend with their kids, look for an external validating measure, like grades in school, to make themselves feel better. This leads to their children feeling more pressure in academic areas than ever before.

"It's a measurable gauge," says Toni Liebman. "If their kids do well in school, that means, at least in their minds, that they as parents are doing their job well."

How to Decide if Now's the Time to Have Them

Ann Landers once said, "You don't need to learn all of life's lessons the hard way. Listen to someone who's been there." For those readers contemplating adding children to their Third Career, here are some issues to mull over. The thing all the parents we asked agreed upon was that the decision about when to start a family was the most momentous one of their married lives. Whether now is the right time for you will be clearer if you answer the following questions honestly:

- What are your reasons for wanting children? Are they compatible with your partner's?

- How will children change your day-to-day schedule? Are you ready and eager to make those adjustments, or will the changes seem more like a sacrifice?

- Will children cause a financial strain in your life? Are you willing to accept the cutting back that might be necessary?

- Are you prepared to deal with the inevitable complications children bring with them? Have you thought about the "what if's"? What if your child is sick on the day you have a business trip scheduled? What if your child has special needs or problems that demand more time than you expected? What if your job gets more demanding—and exciting—when you have one—or two—toddlers at home?[7]

And finally—

- How comfortable are you with your answers to all these questions?

"Kids are not the right decision for everyone," says Carol, 30, and an office manager. "Fred and I are so used to the way things are that to have a child now would totally interrupt our lifestyle. If we want to get up and go, we just do. Of course we are responsible for our six dogs, two dozen chickens and our newest addition, a goat. But that's certainly not the same as having children!"

And in contrast..."I could never imagine my life without children," says Pat, a 35-year-old computer programmer and the mother of four. "There was never a question of whether to have children—just of how many. Sure, we've been through some murderously difficult times—four times the terrible two's and four kids with chicken pox at the same time. The house is messy ten times more than it's neat. Tired is my natural state, and I'm constantly worried about money. But when it's quiet and I lie in bed at night and the kids are snug and sleeping, I know I wouldn't trade my life for anyone's."

WHO'S MINDING THE KIDS?

From the time your baby is in the womb until he can answer the phone, work the microwave and be comfortable waiting alone for you to return, there are important child care problems to be solved. The decision to hand off our children is one of the most difficult decisions Three-Career Couples with kids have to make. How can we not be concerned, having grown up in an era when past studies of Anna Freud, daughter of Sigmund, concluded that children of employed mothers inevitably wound up with what she termed maternal deprivation; and guru Benjamin Spock advised for years that children need mothers who stay at home? With the acceptance of the Three-Career Couple as the new permanent reality comes the next equally challenging decision: To whom should we entrust our precious children while we are not at home?

According to author Sally Wendkos Olds, there are five basic options for child care:

1) parental care with staggered hours

2) care by a relative or close friend

3) a full-time babysitter or housekeeper

4) family day care

5) group care: day care center, nursery school, company-sponsored child care program, before- and after-school programs

"Most parents do not confine themselves to only one form of care," Ms. Olds explains. "They are more likely to use instead a combination of different arrangements. The trick is finding—and keeping—good child care."[8]

Who cares for children when mothers work? Of the 7.4 million children under age five who are the youngest among their siblings and whose mothers worked in 1990—

- 48% used out-of-home nonrelative care (20 percent used family child care where a neighbor usually cared for the child in his or her own home, and 28 percent used a child care center, preschool or nursery school)[9]

- 47% used the care of relatives (28 percent were cared for by parents in staggered shifts; 19 percent by other relatives—predominantly grandparents—in the child's home or a relative's home)

- 3% relied on the care of a nonrelative in the child's home

These numbers showed a decline between 1965 and 1990 in all forms of relative care (62 to 47 percent) and an increase in all forms of nonrelative care (37 to 51 percent) and center-based care (6 to 28 percent).[10]

In other countries around the world, governments provide paid, job-protected parental leaves to let mothers and/or fathers be with their children in the important early months and high-quality, subsidized child care when the parents return to work.

You can always count on Sweden to make the United States look like a Third World country when it comes to matters humane and life-enhancing. Time and time again, programs we believe to be economically unfeasible, they successfully put into practice. In Sweden, both parents can take a childbirth leave for nine months and receive 90 percent of one parent's wages. Until the baby is a year old, they receive smaller benefits. Then for the next six months their leave is unpaid but job-protected. Incredibly, they may work a six-hour day until the child is eight years old.

In Italy, women may take a job-protected leave for six months and receive pay equal to the average wage female workers earn. Then they're allowed another leave, unpaid but job-protected, for one year. French women receive job-protected maternity leaves of six weeks before a baby is born and ten weeks afterward. Until this year, our own record was shameful. Of 100 industrialized countries, the U.S. was the only one without a national policy for parental leave or child care.

The Family and Medical Leave Act, the first bill signed into law by President Bill Clinton, represents a significant step in the advocacy of workplace rights. The new law entitles workers in organizations of 50 or more employees to up to 12 weeks a year of unpaid leave for: birth, adoption or placement in foster care of a child; care of a child, spouse or parent with a serious health condition; or the employee's own serious health condition.

Employees are entitled to the same or equivalent position when returning to work, and health benefits, if offered, must continue during the leave.

Although the law will cover only about 40 percent of America's workforce, and many who are eligible may be unable to afford the benefit since the leaves are unpaid, it still marks a first step in addressing critical work-family issues. Hopefully, this law will pave the way for comparable action on child care, for which our record lags far behind other countries.

In 1986, almost 40 percent of Swedish preschoolers of working mothers were in subsidized child care programs. And more than half the infants, toddlers and preschoolers in France, Italy and Spain received subsidized child care because their mothers were at work. In contrast, the figures for subsidized child care in this country are negligible.[11]

MAKING THE RIGHT CHOICE

Admittedly, some of the facts and findings on child care in this country seem grim. But this does not mean that quality care can't be found. Following are three examples of Three-Career Couples who made the "right" choice in child care, based on their individual needs, budgets and lifestyles.

For Melanie and Glenn, their child care dilemma was settled by their mothers before they even thought of who would be minding their baby when they went to work. "We were at a family barbecue," remembers Glenn, 37 and a lawyer, "when all of a sudden both our mothers came over, with hands on hips, attacking in unison, demanding to know how we were planning to raise their grandchild. Melanie was six months pregnant at the time, and we still had no answer to give them. Not to worry—they already worked everything out."

"They were incredible," adds Melanie, 35 and an office manager of a law firm. "My mom, who is widowed, set aside the first part of the week for the baby. She would come on Monday morning, she told us, and move in until Wednesday evening. Then my mother-in-law would take over Thursday and Friday, as a "day worker," so she could go home in the evenings to be with my father-in-law. She refused to accept any money. My mom was comfortable taking a salary because she was alone and needed the income. The whole thing sounded pretty amazing to Glenn and me, and that's just how it's been for the past eight years—absolutely amazing."

"My first choice in child care was not family day care," says Marla, 30, a nurse's aide. "The first time I took my two-year-old daughter to visit Mrs. Berry's home around the corner, my stomach was in knots. But my husband and I had agreed that a full-time babysitter was too expensive, so we decided to give it a try. As soon as I stepped foot into the house and watched Amanda's reaction, I knew it was going to be okay. Mrs. Berry was so cheerful; Amanda immediately felt comfortable with her. Within a minute she let go of my hand and walked over to the three other two-year-olds in the den who were having a snack. I had come prepared with a list of questions and things to look for; everything checked out positively. But more than that, Mrs. Berry's self-assurance and obvious love for the children in her home made me feel good about being there. I admit that if our budget weren't so tight, I wouldn't have chosen this for Amanda, but now six months later I think that having to give up our babysitter was a blessing in disguise."

Grandma as Caregiver:
The Wisest Choice for Love or Money?

Deciding on whether to pay a relative can be a sticky situation. For care of preschoolers whose mothers are employed, 39 percent pay relatives. According to a 1990 *Redbook* survey, 43 percent of those who used an unpaid relative or friend for child care experienced high levels of stress (compared to 32 percent who paid a relative or friend, 31 percent who used a day care center and 27 percent who employed a nonlive-in babysitter).[12] Before making the decision, it is important to consider: Can you afford to pay? Does the caregiver need the income? Would she be working at another paid job if she wasn't caring for your children?

If you don't pay your caregiver with money, there are other ways to reciprocate. It could be dinner out in her favorite restaurant ("Grandma, are you sure you don't want to choose McDonald's?"), a surprise gift for no reason (Remember that hat your mother admired in the store window?) or a special favor ("Okay, Mom, you're off the hook; Aunt Betty can stay with me for the weekend she's in town. And if that doesn't show you my appreciation for your babysitting, nothing ever will!")

And confessions from a third mom, trying to keep everybody happy—"What's right for one child is not necessarily right for another," says 29-year-old Lorraine, a special education teacher. "We found that out right in our own family. When Brian was born five years ago, we hired a lovely woman to come to the house and take care of him while Charlie and I were at work. That worked out great until he was old enough for nursery school. But with Katy it was different. From the time she was a toddler we knew she needed more stimulation. She got cranky more easily than Brian ever did and was only happy when there was lots of activity around her. Finally we agreed to ship her out for more action. We found a woman in the neighborhood who ran a small family day care center in her home for a few preschool children. For Katy, this has been a dream come true. And for us, it's a lesson in flexibility."

Chants to Handle the Guilt of "Not Being There" When the Kids Get Home from School

For those moments when you're at work and you're positive all good parents of school-age children are at home supervising homework and preparing vegetable soup from scratch, try repeating whichever one of these mantras suits you best:

1) My family knows why I'm here—and knows I'm out of here in five seconds if they need me.

2) I'd put my kids up against those of stay-at-home moms in the mental health olympics any day.

3) I am honestly doing the very best job I can at home and at work.

4) There'd be no summer camp, braces, karate lessons or piano in the house if I weren't working.

5) The happier and more fulfilled I am, the better a parent I can be.

6) If I quit work today, the frustrated, overbearing woman who'd open the door at 3 p.m. would not improve my children's life.

7) What I am sacrificing by not being at home has positively impacted on the reliability, independence and self-confidence I see in my children.

8) My presence at home will not automatically eliminate my children's problems; in fact it would probably just replace them with different ones.

9) I am not a superhero. I cannot do everything. My best is pretty good.

MORNING MADNESS

The well-oiled machine of the Three-Career Couple never breaks down as often as it does between 7 and 8 a.m. Within the space of an hour we have to get ready for work, get cranky kids off to day care and to school, make breakfast, prepare lunch, plan dinner—and do it all while setting a positive, confidence-building tone for the rest of the day. No matter how abrupt, moody or preoccupied your natural morning state might be, when that alarm rings you're center stage without the benefit of a warm-up. You're harried, and you haven't yet dealt with a health emergency, quieted a tantrum or coped with a troublesome car. Taking for granted a good night's sleep, a cooperative spouse and a willingness to preplan, we can guarantee a less problematic start to the day if you would follow these suggestions.

1) You don't want to hear this, but you know it's true. By waking up 30 minutes earlier than you do now you will allow yourself the luxury of a more leisurely paced shower and the opportunity of getting dressed before waking the rest of the house. It doesn't mean you still

won't have to brush your teeth in the shower and finish your makeup on the expressway, but at least you'll be down to tending to just five things at once.

2) Give each family member his or her own alarm clock. Set them to go off ten minutes earlier than you really want them up. Then, if necessary, start calling, tickling, splashing water, shaking, raising the volume on the radio, pulling off the covers and turning on the lights. Try to remember that just because you're on fast forward doesn't mean your kids have to be. If they're really dawdling, consider working on getting them to bed earlier.

3) Designate one spot where everything that's leaving the house in the morning is kept (notes, lunch boxes, briefcases, etc.). Make sure everyone checks that spot before leaving.

4) Try to establish some pleasant rituals like reading the comics, sharing schedule information such as who's picking up whom and what afterschool activities are planned, and create your own good-bye routines (pet names, secret handshake, certain number of kisses, etc.).

5) The night before when laying out the kids' clothes, don't ask, "What do you want to wear?" but rather, "Do you want to wear your blue pants or your brown ones?" Giving open-ended choices is just asking for trouble.

6) Stay calm. Sitters will cancel, kids will wake up with fevers, cars will not start. Big deal if the outfit your child picked out clashes or he left after eating only two bites of his cereal. Don't engage in power struggles. Early mornings are not the time for rational, prime-time negotiating, and starting the day on the wrong foot will keep you off balance till dinner.

DECOMPRESSING—MAKING THE TRANSITION BETWEEN WORK AND HOME

Author Sally Wendkos Olds suggests some strategies for easing the reentry from the harried work world to the hectic home front. Going cold turkey without decompressing can ruin the entire evening. Try them out, and see if any fit your situation. While this might not be the first time you've seen some of these, maybe it'll be the first time you act on them. Just like weight loss is more a result of your motivation and commitment than the uniqueness of any particular diet, so it's true that any of the following advice will work if you're serious about making it happen.

- Before you leave work, make a list of the things you'll have to deal with the following day; this helps keep your mind free of work problems once you're home with your family.
- Get off the bus or train earlier than you have to and walk the rest of the way home. If you're driving, detour by a park for a ten-minute stroll.
- Exercise for 15 to 30 minutes: run, walk, bicycle, swim or jump rope—either alone or with any family members who want to join you.
- Tell everyone you have to watch the news on TV and will be available in half an hour. You can all view it together as you unwind, or you can go into a room by yourself.
- Take a 15-minute bath or shower—with or without your baby or small child.
- Lie down for 15 minutes to half an hour, issuing an open invitation to family members who want to tell you their news while you're stretched out. This lying down break may just calm the children, too.
- Change from work clothes into jeans, a caftan or whatever else spells relaxation for you. If you're not going out or

expecting guests, you might even get into your pajamas and robe. In some families, everyone does this early—and then the day's laundry is done before bed.

- Put out some raw vegetables or cheese and crackers right away so you can relax and serve dinner later.
- Put a favorite record on the stereo and listen to music while you look at the mail.
- Meditate for 15 minutes.[13]

DINNERTIME

A 1990 *New York Times* poll revealed that 74 percent of the 555 adults it surveyed rated eating dinner together with their family as a priority of utmost importance. Eighty percent said they'd eaten dinner together the previous night, a remarkable testament to the sanctity of this coming-together time.[14]

"Dinner is our everyday opportunity to strengthen our relationships," says Joan, a 36-year-old account executive and mother of two. "Before I tuned into the importance of this time in reestablishing our children's sense of closeness and belonging, I was ridiculously hung up with what and how much my kids ate. I bought into the myth that to be a good parent means ensuring that a well-rounded diet gets into each and every child each and every day. Now when my kids refuse to eat something I've prepared, I let it go. Dinnertime is about sharing experiences, planning for the weekend and catching up. I'm embarrassed at all the time I wasted trying to force feed my 100 percent healthy kids. And how personally I took it when they wouldn't touch my meat loaf or taste my clam chowder. How did I forget that I didn't learn to eat pork chops, onions or broccoli until I was 20—and no longer *had to*."

Whether you have to postpone your hungry family's dinner with carrot sticks and dip or settle for just dessert together if one of you is delayed, building in a daily 25 to 30 minutes of uninterrupted togetherness is one of the best things you can do to cement family bonds. If dinnertime in your house is fragmented and less than satisfactory, see if any of these tips can satisfy your appetite for a more ideal dinnertime experience.

- We promise that this is the last time we'll say it—plan ahead. Eliminate tedious daily decision making. It's a lot of work at first, but developing a monthly meal planner that includes a variety of home-cooked and convenience foods, provisions for an occasional night out and seasonal specialties is totally worth the effort in the long run.

- Take the easy way out. Your microwave is your best friend for defrosting, steaming vegetables and cooking the fast foods made specifically for busy families.

- Divvy up the work load. Everyone is eating, so everyone should contribute to making dinner happen. Rotate tasks weekly to keep arguments at a minimum.

- Allow no interruptions. Turn on the answering machine and turn off the TV. Put away the newspaper and video games. Mandating dinner an interruption-free zone will instill in your kids how important it is to keep this time pure.

- Leave unpleasantries for later. The dinner table is a place for praise and positive messages—not a battleground where disappointed expectations, unmet needs and punishments are discussed.

- Go with the flow. It's not important if your new dish is not a unanimous success. Remember that Weight Watchers is full of former kids who used to be members of the "clean plate club."

- Teach the dynamics of real conversation. It's worth a few minutes to clip an interesting article, think of a current issue or come up with a question for everyone to answer. Yes, it's contrived, and maybe they'll think your ideas are corny, but if you hit it right the interaction can be delicious.

What about, "If there were a fire and you could pack one thing, what would it be?" "What was the best thing that happened to you today? The biggest disaster?" "If you could move anywhere in the world, where would it be?" "What do you like best about ____? (choose someone at the table)" "What should we buy ____ (grandma, aunt, babysitter, etc.) for _____ (birthday, anniversary, Christmas, etc.)?"

■ Surprise them all! Try finding the time to serve a new food or an old food in an unusual way. Set up a picnic on a blanket in the family room or put up a buffet table. Make an "unbirthday" party for everyone, or celebrate an ethnic holiday that's not your own. Even if it's a bust, it'll get them out of the midweek stupor.

■ Include laughter. The rest of the day moves so quickly that it would be wonderful if dinnertime were an oasis of relaxation. Sharing funny incidents, jokes, tongue twisters and comics can supply badly needed relief from tension.

■ Keep trying. This list suggests goals to aspire to and experiences to emulate—not a seven-day-a-week rigid recipe for joyous dining. Change takes time, but the results of a warmer, relaxing dinner hour are worth it.

WHEN THE WEEK ENDS

We've talked about the benefits of remaining flexible and being open to new ideas, but there is no greater boon to family bonds and future memories than the unique routines each family establishes. For kids, keeping some activities at the same time each day—dinner at 6, bedtime at 8—and some weekly events on a set schedule—storytime at the library every Thursday afternoon, family meetings on Sunday at 4—helps them to feel a sense of order in their lives. Parents also rely on built-in family routines—from watching the nightly news after dinner to cuddling at bedtime—as their anchor. Looking forward to weekend routines—Saturday afternoon family outings, Sunday morning breakfasts in bed, Sunday dinners on paper plates—can help them get through even the most turbulent week. For three-career families, routines are often the key to keeping life on track.

For Kathy and Larry, both police officers in the same precinct, the hardest time of the week was Sunday morning when one worked and the other was trying to catch up on some sleep. "When the kids were four and six, we thought they could take care of themselves for a few hours if one of us was upstairs sleeping after a long shift," explains Kathy. "Unfortunately, they didn't understand that no reason other than a life-threatening one was good enough to disturb us. There was always someone running upstairs to tattle on the other. The proverbial last straw happened one Sunday, after a particularly tough night on the street, when our daughter shook me awake, waved the newspaper in my face and asked if I could please check to see if any of her lottery tickets were listed. I knew we had to come up with a new routine. The solution: bribery. I paid each child four dollars to babysit the other while I slept, with instructions that if either came upstairs for any reason other than an emergency, neither of them would get paid. I admit, it took bribe money to convince them to let me sleep, but for eight dollars it was worth it!"

"The best thing about Wednesday is there are only two more days till the weekend," says Jackie, a mother of three and the owner of a retail candy store. "Now that the kids are older and they often have plans of their own, we make a point that everyone promise to keep Sunday free. Wednesday night we work out our weekend itinerary. We try to do one nice indoor activity together every month in the winter—we either go to a museum, a sports event or a movie. When the weather is warm, we head for the zoo, the beach or rent bikes for a few hours. Everyone is not equally thrilled with the choice of activity all the time (sometimes we invite a friend if the protests grow too loud), but we're satisfied to be batting 700."

"For me, the best part of the weekend are the few hours of extra sleep Saturday morning," says Jon, Jackie's husband. "Since the kids were real little we've had a Saturday morning crate full of things for them to do when they get up. It's full of small individual-size cereal boxes, some books, video games and toys. The noise level is not exactly conducive to sleeping late, but at least Jackie and I get to loll about and spend some time together."

Parenting routines also instill a teamwork attitude in the family. Even if the kids find some of the routines silly (like Myra and Ben's Friday night games of gin rummy—loser drives the car pools on Saturday morning) or unfair (like Robin and Joe's weekly meetings behind a "do not disturb" bedroom door to discuss "parenting matters") or funny ("Do you believe this? Mom has to work late, so Dad is leading our Brownie meeting!")—they can feel the cooperative family spirit behind their parents' actions. The foundation for this cooperative spirit is communication, says Dr. Mary Rose Paster, a psychologist who works with children, adolescents and families in her New York private practice. "Given that there is a requirement for more flexibility in a three-career family, the roles cannot be as rigid. Parents should have ground rules that they make and enforce together. There has to be a game plan, but the system must be flexible."

WICKED STEPMOTHER? NOT ME!

Once a rarity, the stepfamily is today a growing reality. Statistics show that one out of every two marriages is likely to end in divorce. For American women, ages 15 to 44, seven out of ten divorcees will remarry within five years of their divorce. These figures, according to author James D. Eckler in his book

Step-by-Stepparenting, add up to 1,300 American stepfamilies with children under 18 forming every day![15] As if juggling career, home, marriage and family weren't challenging enough, the stepparent has an extra ball in the air: stepchildren.

"As a stepmother, I try even harder with the kids than if they were my own," says Wendy, 38, a social worker and stepmom to three boys, ages 14, 11 and 9. "I know it's hard sometimes for them to accept me, and I try to give them their space. One of the things that has worked in building our relationship is spending time at home with them alone when their dad is not there. I try to schedule times away from my practice when I know that one or more of the boys will be home.

"Recently the 11-year-old came home from school with a pet mouse; no one had volunteered to take the classroom pet home for the school vacation, so he finally did—after his father had flatly forbidden it. To make matters worse, the mouse escaped from its cage and was lost somewhere in the house where no one could find it. Our afternoon together became a joint search for this mouse, with my promise that I wouldn't tell his father. We finally bought traps to catch the mouse, and at 3 a.m. victory was ours.

"His dad never did find out about our secret, and the experience together created a bond between us that I know will be lasting. It has also reinforced my decision to spend as much time as possible at home with the boys—one-on-one—to develop a special relationship with each one of them."

The important lesson for Wendy, says Dr. Paster, is that the experience with her stepson gave them an opportunity to problem solve together and to come up with a positive solution. However, she cautions stepparents not to encourage situations in which secrets are kept from their spouse. The role of a stepmother, as in Wendy's case, should not be to tattle on her stepson, but to encourage him to tell his father the truth.

Alliances between stepparents and children are often fragile in the early stages of creating a stepfamily. The intrusion of a new person into the family is often threatening to children and resentment is not uncommon. To build a more positive stepfamily relationship, Dr. Paster offers these commonsense guidelines:

- Spend as much time with stepchildren as possible. Make an effort to learn about the children—what they like, fear, etc.

- Be a friend and a good listener, without being judgmental. Never betray their confidences, and encourage honesty and open communication.

- Be honest and reliable. Don't make promises you can't keep.

- Don't compete with the biological parent. Avoid situations in which children are forced to face conflicts of loyalty. If possible, establish a working relationship with the natural parent to reinforce a positive spirit and an absence of competition.

- Show affection, but be sensitive to how they receive it. Let children set the pace; you can't force closeness until they are ready.

- Communicate, communicate, communicate. Acknowledge that a stepfamily is not always the easiest living arrangement and that resentment at times is understandable. Reassure the children that your job is not to take the place of another parent, but rather to enhance the family. Talk with your spouse about issues that concern the children: education, recreation, discipline, finances. Disagree over issues in privacy; it's important for the children to see you as united.

- Create a family spirit—through shared activities, family problem solving and decision making.

SUMMING IT UP

On a gut level the reality is that you're doing, on a part-time basis, the parenting job that someone, perhaps just one generation ago, used to do full time. No way can you be on top of every situation with the same level of concentration. But what Three-Career Couples are learning is that the families they're creating have their own unique strengths—strengths that develop precisely because of these same demands put upon them today. Your life can only be improved if you:

- Worry only when necessary. Not every problem your child experiences is related to your three careers. Growing up would be painful even if Betty Crocker were your mother. Recognize that childhood is full of phases and stages, and they all pass with time.

- Do only what you can. While you should make time every day to spend together (dinnertime is ideal) don't try to live up to fantasies, where everyone seems to be doing everything perfectly in sync.

- Make your family unique. Plan activities, and if they're successful, make them traditions. (Go into the country and watch the leaves turn color every autumn; take pictures each year in front of the same vacation spot; work together to prepare a holiday meal for company.)

- Take pride in what you've accomplished. Talk about your day and share your careers with your children. They will absorb your sense of competence and fortify themselves for the difficult world ahead.

- Stay optimistic. All you can do is the best you can do. Kids are infinitely forgiving of our mistakes, and rare is the problem without a solution.

CHICKEN POX? NOT ON MY DEADLINE!
Handling Unexpected Crises

The sky is falling, the sky is falling.
Chicken Little

There's an old Yiddish proverb that says, "Man makes plans and God laughs." No one is exempt from falling into the unseen potholes of life that sometimes make our journey such a bumpy one. And the driving skills needed to find our way back into moving traffic had better be readily accessible. By definition, emergencies are unforeseen combinations of circumstances that call for immediate action. Some can be solved with a little ingenuity: "When my two-year-old stuck a baked bean up each nostril and I broke them in half when I tried getting them out with my fingers, thank God my husband thought of putting pepper under his nose. He sneezed them right out." Others need a more reliable approach: "It seems like there're at least two nights a month I have to devote to my parents' paperwork. Whether it's fighting an insurance claim that's been denied, researching a new drug that one specialist recommends and another is leery about or coordinating doctor appointments so that either my wife or I can be there to hear what's going on—there's always a situation cropping up that demands quick, undivided attention." Some are thankfully one-shot deals; others are long-term situations.

"I got so paranoid after Jake got into the cabinet under the sink and started squirting liquid dishwashing detergent down the baby's mouth that we just spent $450 to babyproof our home," says Aileen, a 37-year-old teacher and mother of two. "We have potty locks and cabinet latches, stove knob covers and venetian blind cord shorteners, fire extinguishers and rail extenders—all to give us peace of mind when we're not at home."

"The school nurse called to tell me Laura seriously injured her foot and needed to see a doctor right away," says Linda, a program director of a national advocacy organization that recently moved its offices from a 15-minute suburban car ride to an hour train commute into New York City. "Jerry hadn't left for work yet, but he had to teach a class in two hours. He wound up driving Laura into the city stretched out in the back of the car. He hopped out, took a cab to class and I drove her back to Connecticut to our orthopedist. No doubt Laura was in pain—but I looked a lot worse."

"I just got the third phone call this week from my mother in Florida. This time my job was to figure out a way to explain to her the workings of the new bank statement she'd just received. 'Your dad just doesn't have the head for this stuff anymore, and I never did,' she said. What am I supposed to do?" says Judy, 43, a health club administrator and mother of an infant daughter. "Every week there's another situation that's becoming too much for them to handle. They leave the doctor's office without understanding or questioning what he said. They forgot to pay the phone bill and completely panicked when the phone went dead. My dad has had three minor fender benders—all in the supermarket parking lot—in the last six months. And I hear this tone in my mother's voice, so low and depressed, that I know I could make it better if only I were there. But the baby has bronchitis, and my husband'll have a fit if I fly down to see them so soon after my last trip. I feel so guilty being 1,500 miles away, but we just can't afford all these trips."

Companies are losing four billion dollars annually due to absenteeism caused by child and elder care problems, according to Irving Edwards, CEO of Plaza Nurses Agency, a business of over 1,000 professional caregivers: "With more women in key management positions, men taking on family responsibilities and the longevity of the elderly, most working people are feeling the stressful squeeze of balancing a job with family care—especially when emergencies arise."

THE FLU? IT CAN'T BE!

"When I took this job, I thought I had all my bases covered," says Maryann, 34, and a sportswear buyer for a chain of retail stores. "I hired a young, wonderful live-in babysitter to care for my three kids. The first time Ben came down with a bad virus and ran a fever of 104, I fell apart. I never anticipated how difficult it would be to leave him when he was feeling so sick. I stayed home the first day to show Doreen, who wasn't a mother yet herself, how to handle him when he's cranky and uncomfortable. The next day I had a meeting I couldn't miss. As soon as it was over, I raced right home. The next few days, while Ben was still burning up, I just couldn't leave him. One week later, Emily caught Ben's virus, and it started all over again. Needless to say, it was an awful month. It made me realize that as well organized as I think I am, there are some things like sickness and accidents you have no control over that force you to rearrange your priorities."

Until the day chicken pox becomes extinct, germs are no longer contagious and sick children don't want their mommies to comfort them (women are far more likely than men to take days without pay to care for a sick child—24 percent of women compared to 4 percent of men),[1] working parents and sick children will be a major thorn in business's side. In a *Fortune* magazine study of two-earner families with children 12 years old and under, 57 percent of the respondents said that finding care for a sick child was a major problem.[2] Another study at Adolph Coors Company found sick child care problems to be the leading cause of employee absence.[3]

To take time off for a sick child, parents resort to a variety of strategies. Ellen Galinsky, in her report, Education Before School: Investing in Quality Child Care, cites one example of a large (unnamed) hospital, in which

- 36% of parents took days off without pay,
- 30% took personal sick days and
- 24% took vacation days

to stay home with sick children.[4]

"Every morning when I wake the kids, if one feels warm or her coloring doesn't look right, I get this momentary panic," says Sara, 34, and a customer service representative for a department store. "Before they even open their eyes, I'm worried about what I'm going to do if they're sick—even though Jamie may feel warm because my hands are cold or because she sleeps with her head squished into her pillow. There's nothing worse than finding out five minutes before I'm ready to head out the door that I'm not going anywhere. Last year, when Stacy had the flu for two weeks, I missed a week's pay. What was my choice? I'm still a mom first."

Concerns among employers over absenteeism due to sick children have prompted the formation of a number of company-sponsored, sick child care programs throughout the country.

IDS Financial Services, a subsidiary of American Express, surveyed employees and discovered that only 25 percent were satisfied with their sick child care arrangements, and 75 percent had no safety net. They started a sick child care program in 1988 that, although expensive, offers employees two reliable options when their backs are against the wall. They provide a trained caregiver in the child's own home (for $13.50 an hour) or place the child in a specially designated section of a local medical center (for $50 a day). Based on parent evaluations, satisfaction has been high among users of the program.[5]

In 1989 a group of seven New York City companies launched a one-year pilot program for emergency child care services for their employees. They contracted with two home healthcare agencies to provide services for situations when a child was mildly ill, when a caregiver was suddenly unavailable or when school or a child care program was not in session and parents had to work. Each company had its own policy for reimbursing the fee of $13 an hour. Since its inception, eight additional companies have joined the New York group.[6]

Chicken Soup in Minneapolis is a child care center for mildly ill children of employees in a number of companies in the Twin Cities. The center is divided into one room for respiratory illnesses, one for gastrointestinal problems and one for chicken pox. Charges are normally $35 a day, of which many participating companies subsidize 50 percent or more.[7]

The success of these initiatives has varied. Some parents may be unwilling to bring their sick children to a strange location or are reluctant to have a stranger come into their home. Nevertheless, these programs mark a growing awareness of the importance of this work-family issue.

Realizing that parents may want to stay home with sick children, some companies are reversing their sick leave policies. An inspiring example is Goodyear Tire & Rubber Company, which in their 1992 resource guide on work and family issues, grants excused time off with pay for up to one week (at management's discretion) for a sick child or spouse. A Conference Board Survey of 521 large companies found that 58 percent offer sick family leave (59 percent of it unpaid).

But your reality might be quite different. A 1990 survey of 188 Fortune 1000 companies found that fewer than 5 percent had specifically designated family, sick or emergency days. Typically, one or two days are added to an existing sick leave policy or permission is granted to use sick leave for family purposes.[8]

"It's beyond frustrating when the kids get sick," says Jane (the exercising insurance broker from Chapter 2). "I can't afford to take sick days every time one of them has the flu or strep throat, but they're too young to stay home alone. My saving grace has been 'Aunt Sally' who lives down the street. She's a retired widow who has become like a grandmother to my children. She invites them over after school to bake cookies and knits sweaters for them on their birthdays. The first time my daughter had the flu and I was in a panic because I had an important client coming in that day, Aunt Sally offered to stay with her. My daughter was thrilled. They spent the whole day doing jigsaw puzzles and watching game shows on TV. Since then she's been my cover when the kids get sick. On the weekends I take her to do her errands since she no longer drives. It's a magical swap that just sort of happened. Truthfully, when the kids are ill, I think they'd rather be nursed by her than me!"

Handling the sudden sick child crisis begins, once again, with advance planning (What else is new?). Just as you prepare your kids for "what if. . ." emergency situations ("What would you do if there were a fire? If someone rang the doorbell? If there were a power failure?"), you must also develop contingency plans for yourself. It's important to know your resources.

- Are you lucky enough to work for a progressive company that has provisions for employees when their children get sick?
- If not, does your employer allow you to use your personal days when the kids are sick? What is the policy—if any—regarding sick children?
- How flexible is your job? Can you bring a mildly sick child to work with you? Can you bring work home with you? Can you and your spouse split the workday so that each one works half the day and is home half the day to take care of your sick child?

If you have to get to work, can you call a relative, a neighbor or a friend (one with whom your child is comfortable, of course) to cover for you? Are there any local agencies you trust? The more you plan, the more easily you'll be able to deal with emergency situations—not only a sudden case of chicken pox, but a stalled car or a cancelled babysitter as well.

HELP! OUR NANNY JUST QUIT!

A breakdown in child care is right up there with sick children and complications with elderly parents as the most traumatic of crisis situations described by the couples we interviewed.

"We were finishing breakfast when the phone rang," recalls Marla (the nurse's aide with a two-year-old daughter whom we met in Chapter 5). "It was Mrs. Berry calling to say she was sick and couldn't watch Amanda that day. It was 7 a.m.; what was I supposed to do? My husband had already left for work, my parents were away on vacation and at that hour I didn't have a clue where to turn. I had no choice but to call my supervisor to tell her I wouldn't be into work that day. I didn't exactly get a gold star for such last minute notice."

Whether a caregiver cancels or quits, is sick or unavailable, sudden child care problems are murderously aggravating. When parents were asked in the *Fortune* magazine study of two-earner families with children 12 years old and under how many times in the last three months they had to make special arrangements because of a child care breakdown, 40 percent responded at least once, and 25 percent said between two and five times. The study also found that the more often parents had to make special child care arrangements, the more likely they were to report stress-related health problems—including shortness of breath, a pounding or racing heart, back or neck pains, overeating, drinking more alcohol than usual, smoking more or taking more tranquilizers.[9] If there's a lesson to be learned from these findings, it's that we need to protect ourselves and our children with back-up plans for the times when our primary plans collapse.

For Susan (the nursery school teacher with chronic PMS of Chapter 1), the solution has been teaming up with a friend in a "backup partnership." "Shari is a caterer and works evenings and weekends," Susan explains. "She's usually home during the day, and I'm around when she's working. Our deal is to cover for each other in emergencies. If one of my kids gets sick at school, the school nurse knows to call Shari. If she's unavailable on a Saturday afternoon to drive her kids to soccer practice, I'm the designated chauffeur. There's no more choosing between missing work and abandoning our kids—we know we always have each other. The two of us are on opposite schedules—it's amazing we find time to be friends!"

Backup for Ellen, 31, a mother of two-year-old twin boys and a copywriter for a public relations firm, came from an understanding boss (and a mother herself) who instituted a policy that allowed employees who found themselves in emergency situations to work from home—as long as their performance kept up to expected standards. "No one ever takes advantage of it," says Ellen. "But knowing I don't have to get hysterical if my babysitter doesn't show one morning is the best perk of my job. It's only happened once, and I got my work done while the boys were napping and then when they were watching *Sesame Street.* While my kitchen table might not be the most inspiring place to create genius, I was so grateful not to lose the day's work that I produced some neat stuff that day."

VACATION TIME—BUT NOT FOR EVERYONE!

Jingle bells and a ho ho ho! Holiday time means school vacations and euphoric children. But when the kids are off and you're not, it's just more problems for the Three-Career Couple. Obviously, in a perfect world the solution would be to schedule your vacation days to coincide with school breaks. But in the real world, even if your company doesn't yet have a built-in, back-up child care program, there are practical and creative alternatives available. All of the following ideas may not apply to your situation, but since they are proven solutions from the lives of other Three-Career Couples, maybe picking and choosing and combining and adapting their ideas will help you create your own ideal solution.

1) Bring your child(ren) to work with you. "I wasn't sure how Roberta would handle it when I showed up with my kids during their winter vacation," confesses Leslie (Roberta's partner at the children's boutique we met in Chapter 3). "She was willing to give it a shot because she knew I had no other alternative. They're too young to stay home alone, and there was no one I felt comfortable leaving them with for such long stretches of time. It turned out that not only were they not in the way, but they loved bringing out merchandise from the back room and straightening up the dressing rooms. They wound up being so helpful—especially during the preholiday

rush—that we offered them money to continue their work for the entire week!"

2) Establish a parent cooperative. A group of five working mothers—all neighbors or acquaintances of neighbors—were trying to figure out what to do with their six-year-olds during spring break. "When I first suggested a cooperative, I wasn't even sure what the word really meant," confesses Ellie, a travel agent. "It was a 70s concept I'd read about but never saw in practice. I was amazed when the idea caught on. Each of us agreed to take off one day during that week and be responsible for all five kids—to plan a fun activity with them and keep them busy till dinner. That gave each of us four full days to work without worry or guilt, confident that our kids were well covered and happy during their vacation. The plan turned out to be a creative success!"

3) Back to that safety net—tap your resources for back-up child care. "My mom has always had a full schedule, crammed with volunteer work, her pottery, two book clubs and yoga," says Adele, 39, a magazine editor. "She and my dad were always so busy that I never thought they'd be available to babysit. But when February school vacation coincided with a major deadline at work, I had no choice but to ask for their help. I could never have anticipated their reaction. Not only were they flattered, they were sincerely thrilled to have some time alone with the kids. The next thing I knew, they made last-minute reservations to take the kids skiing upstate for four days. That left me with the peace of mind I needed to survive that brutal workweek and gave me four incredibly romantic nights alone with Tom—the first time in ten years!"

4) Hire someone for vacation child care. "The housing market was finally picking up when spring vacation snuck up on me," admits Elaine, 40, a real estate broker. "As much

as I wanted to be with the boys, I couldn't afford to take time off. They're old enough to be left alone, but I felt guilty that they'd be disappointed and bored with five whole days without an adult around to take them places. Then I bumped into their former babysitter, home from college on her spring break, and I offered her the job of supervising the boys' activities for the week. She was eager to make the extra money, especially spending time doing the things she likes anyway. We worked out a schedule for the week that included bowling, the planetarium, the arcade and the movies. That week I sold a house I had been working on for months and made my biggest commission ever!"

5) If your child is old (and mature) enough to stay home alone, structure activities to make it feel like a vacation. "My son is 13," says Karlene, 44, a sales person at a retail boutique. "He's at that awkward in-between age, too old for a babysitter but too young to drive and get places on his own. During his spring vacation we were running big sales in the shop, and I couldn't take time off to be with him. So we planned a week for him that satisfied us both. It went something like: Monday he could invite a few friends to come over to play ball (emergency numbers posted on the pad by the phone in case of injury), have lunch (sandwiches made the night before) and watch movies (tapes rented the day before). Tuesday was a stay-at-home day and an opportunity for him to earn money (his idea). Grooming the dog earned him five dollars, cleaning the playroom closet another five. It was also a day to get any schoolwork out of the way. Wednesday he went with a friend (and nonworking mom) to an amusement park. Thursday he walked into town with a friend, they went out to lunch at the pizza parlor and then rented video games to play during the afternoon. And Fri-

day morning he continued playing his favorite video games only to find his dad home by noon, thanks to a quiet day at the office and an urge to spend the afternoon with his son. The bonus for Todd at week's end was how proud he was of living quasi-independently through this vacation. The bonus for me was that I survived letting him!"

PARENTING YOUR PARENTS

According to a 1990 study, Eldercare in the 90s, by Karen Denton, Lois Love and Robert Slate, approximately 30 million elderly persons (65 years and older) in the United States make up 12 percent of the population. By 2030 the figures should jump to 65 million, or 21 percent of the population. The population over the age of 85 is expected to increase 250 percent in this same period.[10] In its 1989 Mother's Day Report, the Older Women's League revealed that 30 percent of American women over 18 will at some time find themselves part of the "sandwich" family.[11] The term "sandwich generation," coined by authors Lois Rosenthal, Alice Priest Shafran and Judith Schwartz in *Sylvia Porter's Personal Finance* magazine, describes those of us caught in the middle of the sandwich, with the bite coming from either our parents and children or our parents and our plans for the future.

For some Three-Career Couples, the feeling might closer resemble that of being pulled apart, tugged at in opposite directions like a wishbone. Acting responsibly for aging parents is a payback for the care they gave us—plus a way of making peace with the people we made war with as adolescents. Fulfilling our obligations to our parents shows the next generation what families do out of love, concern and respect, and ensures (hopefully!) that these values will be perpetuated. The issues are not new, but because people are living longer (Willard Scott's cut-off age to announce birthdays on the *Today Show* is now about 102) and we're choosing to bear children later, millions will soon be facing the crunch.

Our older generation is the healthiest and wealthiest our society has ever produced. Although all people travel through normal growth and development paths, no two people travel exactly the same path at the same time. Accidents, ill health and a spouse dying can accelerate the aging process.

The strain of caring for elderly persons is so great that a few companies in New York City, including American Express and Phillip Morris, have provided a service called Partnership for Eldercare, which offers counseling and seminars for employees who care for elderly parents. One third of the 600 people who signed up for the program (which started in 1988) are caring for relatives long distance. A research study conducted by the partnership estimates that one in five employees in business throughout the country is involved in caring for elderly relatives.[12]

"It wasn't until my mother died that I realized how dependent my father had become," says Terry, 38, a nurse and mother of three. "He wasn't even 70, so I thought I had a few years before I had to worry about taking care of him. I didn't anticipate his depression. The phone would ring in the middle of the night. 'I have chest pains'; 'there's nothing to eat in the house'; 'please understand that if I decide to end my life, it has nothing to do with loving you.' I was a wreck until we came up with a plan to solve the dilemma. I got a crash course in what to do from the many support systems and resource groups I hadn't even known existed. A wonderful private care manager that one of the groups suggested saved my life. All of them did their part in helping to explain the quagmire of Medicaid, living wills, durable power of attorney and my own feelings of incompetence, guilt and anxiety."

Today, although it's not always possible for women to stay home to care for an aging parent, it is still their responsibility to be the caregiver 72 percent of the time.[13] Almost one in three caregivers is the daughter of the care recipient.[14] She will need to lean on her cooperative husband if she has to incorporate this extra responsibility into her already busy life.

We're assaulted by a wide range of emotions when we notice signs of aging in our parents and feel the pressure of their growing dependency. As we see health fail and minds become fragile, there's a sadness, almost a mourning, for a support that's no longer there. Sometimes this grief triggers denial, and we neglect organizing our resources to cope with this new stage. Sometimes it's anger and resentment that surface—at our parents for getting old, at ourselves for not being more adept at juggling their needs with our own. Most of the time it's guilt that's the overriding emotion. Uncomfortable, debilitating, all-consuming guilt for not doing enough to repay them as we should. And for taking time from our family and our work to do such a mediocre job of helping them when they need it the most.

Although each situation is different, here's some good advice—practical, commonsense hints to make sure you're in a state of readiness should an emergency occur. If your parents did the best job they could in raising you, you owe them your best now.

1) The goal is always to keep them independent for as long as possible. Don't be tempted to prematurely take over or take them in. Don't allow them to give in or give up. Allow parents the dignity of conducting their own affairs and making their own decisions. They must always feel their input is important, that they are still in control.

"One of my worst judgment calls was insisting that my mother come and live with us after my dad died," says Ken,

Judy's husband. "I thought I was doing what was best for her, but really it was what was easiest for me. She was left every day by herself, sitting in a strange house without her friends. In two months she packed her bags and moved back to her old neighborhood. I learned that she, not me, knows best what's good for her. Because her vision and her hearing weren't what they used to be, I thought she wasn't capable of being alone. The truth was, I wasn't capable of thinking of her being alone."

2) Have a family meeting. Together decide which family member should be the ultimate decision maker in case of unforeseen circumstances. Distributing the emotional burden and the work among you, your spouse, your own children and your siblings will make the extra load lighter. Everyone can find a job that best fits his or her abilities. There's lots to be divided up—research, financial matters, personal cheerleading, dealing with physicians, insurance forms and the like.

3) Plan one visit to your parents so you can accompany them to their doctor. If the doctor sees your concern, he'll accept your phone calls more readily. Go over all their medications to make sure they're not outdated and unnecessary. Make sure their pharmacist does not dispense medication in difficult-to-open childproof bottles.

4) Check your parents' home for unsafe conditions. Remove slippery scatter rugs. Install nightlights in the bedroom, halls and bathrooms. Arrange ahead for leaf and snow removal. Be sure smoke detectors are working. Lower the hot water temperature to prevent burns. Check electric cords for fraying and outlets for overuse. Investigate alarm options, some of which alert predetermined personnel in an emergency situation.

5) If they live far away, keep your parents involved in your family's affairs—and you in theirs. Videotape family out-

ings and send them to your parents so they can play them back on their own VCR. Send catalogs to help them choose their clothing. Write periodic thank-you notes to their neighbors who might help out with small tasks. Get to know the local Better Business Bureau; should you have questions regarding any business problems, they will be a good resource. Introduce yourself to their banker and establish a rapport. List your name with utility companies to be notified if bills have not been paid so that you can investigate. Since mail carriers are directed to report older people's uncollected mail, instruct the post office to notify you or a trusted neighbor. Have your phone and theirs converted to the most economical service. Use the least expensive times of the day to call, and call regularly. If they trust you will call consistently, they will learn to plan on your assistance. Get an additional copy of their local phone directory to take home with you to use.

6) Prepare ahead with your parents for possible crises. Experts say the best way to prepare for a health crisis is to ask one or both parents a series of "What if..." questions: What if you become disabled? Mentally impaired? What if you have to choose between home care and a nursing home? Since you're forced to react without the luxury of time in a medical emergency, explaining to your parents that one day you may have to make difficult decisions for them and you want the benefit of their preferences, can avoid any extra trauma.

"When my parents first moved to Florida, I never thought to ask any questions about their bank statements, insurance policies, wills or Medicaid paperwork," says Lora, a 40-year-old accountant. "But that was ten years ago. This past Christmas I noticed that both of them were visibly older. I know how reluctant they would be to reveal their finances, but I realized there was too much I didn't know. Not without some stammering and sweating, I got them to agree to record all of their important financial information and to tell me where they keep it. It was a difficult conversation for all of us, but when it was over we all knew we did the right thing."

7) Try to convince your parents of the importance of drawing up a durable power of attorney and a living will. It's a smart move for Three-Career Couples as well—in fact, your doing it may be the way to persuade them to do it. A durable power of attorney authorizes a person (spouse, child) to make decisions on the parents' behalf and authorize an attorney to do the same. It is valid even if an elderly person is not cognizant. Depending on how the document is drawn up, it can refer to specific matters (paying bills, selling property, establishing trusts) or all matters. A living will is a document that allows for parents to choose not to prolong their lives artificially, in the event that they become terminally ill, mentally incompetent or comatose. Lawyers specializing in elder law are a good resource for these affairs.

8) Take advantage of the many resources available to you. Be aware that there are many professionals, books and organizations out there with an understanding and sensitivity for the psychological, financial, legal and medical aspects of what you're going through. Take advantage of them. Call the Eldercare Locator number at 1-800-677-1116 to find the location of the nearest area agency on aging. There are almost 700 such agencies across the country that coordinate and fund more than 20,000 organizations. The American Association of Retired Persons publishes two free pamphlets, "Miles Away and Still Caring" (I.12748) and "A Path for Caregivers" (D12957). Write AARP, P.O. Box 22796, Long Beach, California 90801-5796 and include the title and the stock number.

Care Services for Hire

Innovative entrepreneurs are launching new business ventures to fill our sudden and chronic back-up care needs. We discovered two such ventures (the beginning of many, we hope) that address our concerns.

Caregivers on Call, an offshoot of a home healthcare agency, provides emergency home care for children and aging parents as well as on-site child care programs for companies. During the 1992 tax season in New York, it set up a program at the accounting firm of KPMG Peat Marwick for children ages 1 to 12 whose parents worked overtime on Saturday to finish clients' audits and returns. Caregivers recently added a holiday program to its package of services for companies—a perfect solution for parents whose kids are on vacation while they're not.

Substitute Daughter for Hire is a Florida-based company that answers the prayers of many adult children in the New York area who have aging parents living in the Sunshine State. It offers elderly Floridians a substitute daughter's sensitive, loving care—even though their own children may live hundreds of miles away. Services include taking the elderly parents shopping, accompanying them to the theater or out to dinner or just stopping by once a week to chat over a cup of tea. Former New Yorker and founder of the company, Rhoda Skavroneck, says, "The elderly parents can relax, knowing that someone who cares is only minutes away. When their natural child is not available, their substitute daughter is."

SUMMING IT UP

If kids stayed healthy, babysitters always showed up on time and aging parents were strong, healthy and independent, there'd be no need to read this chapter or take to heart any of the ideas and suggestions found within. But when the baby throws up at 6:30 a.m., school is cancelled for a snow day at 7 a.m. and your elderly, widowed father gets a bad case of the flu, the "new" Three-Career Couple is less likely to fall apart if:

- You have access to appropriate resources. It's helpful to keep a phone book handy with the numbers of back-up babysitters, bail-out friends and relatives, neighbors, agencies, companies, your parents' neighbors, their doctors, local police, and several of their close friends. This way when your car overheats on the expressway, you won't have to depend on the mind you're losing to recall your best friend's phone number.

- You have contingency plans in place. Knowing in advance what you will do if your child wakes up with a fever, your babysitter or caregiver cancels because of a personal emergency or your mom breaks her leg and needs your help, will allow you to appreciate crisisless days and help you better cope with the harder ones. The best defense is a plan of action—ready before you need it.

- You remain flexible. Few days in life are custom-made. If you can remember that a day with a substitute babysitter— even one with a style of her own—won't traumatize your child for life, and that hiring someone to drive your father to the doctor won't seriously interfere with his recovery, then you'll be better able to handle the stress of these complications.

- You can keep a sense of humor. The baked beans were safely removed from your son's nose, your husband made it to his class and your daughter's foot is healing beautifully.

Turn your near-mishaps into the best dinner party stories—everyone appreciates a tragedy averted. If we learn to laugh at ourselves and the never-ending "challenges" that happen when we least expect them, then life's catastrophes may seem just a bit less traumatic.

WE'RE A TWO-EARNER COUPLE, SO WHERE'S ALL THE MONEY?
Financial Considerations

Money may be the husk of many things, but not the kernel. It brings you food, but not appetite; medicine, but not health; acquaintances, but not friends; servants, but not faithfulness; days of joy, but not peace or happiness.

Hendrik Hosen

Moolah. Smackers. Sawbucks. C Notes. The Almighty Dollar. Some marry for it. Some murder for it. Lots of the rest of us get closemouthed and uncomfortable when the subject comes up. In 1981, when *Psychology Today* asked 20,000 people what emotions they associated with money, 71 percent chose anxiety,

52 percent picked depression and 51 percent checked off anger. (More than one answer was allowed.)[1] Money buys us not only food and shelter, but for many, self-worth as well. It influences where and how we live, who we associate with, who we choose as partners. Because, in many instances, it's the final arbiter of value for property, goals, services, even other people, money— or rather worrying about money—is a primary source of stress.

Three-Career Couples brought up in the self-gratifying 60s are at the stage in life when economic pressures are greatest. They were raised and molded by parents who survived the Depression and World War II, who needed little materially (they weren't nobler; there just weren't any microwaves or VCRs to buy) and who can't understand how two hardworking people earning such good money can't seem to get ahead. In the past 25 years the cost of housing has jumped 56 percent and college tuitions have rocketed 87.9 percent. If you bought a home in 1973 your carrying costs equaled 21 percent of your income; by 1987 it was 40 percent.[2]

Money has always been a symbol of power and self-esteem, independence and security. When there's not enough of it to live without worry, women often become stressed and anxious. Men tend to add anger to the pot.

"I would sooner tell you how much I weigh, how often I have sex and the IQs of my kids than talk to you about money," laughs Gail, 35, a medical assistant and mother of two daughters. "It's such a loaded gun. There's tension around the whole topic. If there's too little of it and there's a problem paying the bills, I'm embarrassed and humiliated to work so hard and still find myself owing more than I can comfortably repay. If there's enough, then I'm tense because I'm saving too little or spending too frivolously. We're not talking about dining in restaurants with linen napkins here. It's extra spending on the house—it's more the maintenance and upkeep than decorating that kills me. There's too much of my mom's stinginess in me;

even though I've always earned a salary, while her sense of security hinges entirely on my dad's job."

"I hate talking to Gail about money," says her husband Richard, 37, and a jeweler. "To me numbers are reliable. You make up budgets with them. You plan for the future with them. What you do with the money you earn should be cut and dry. It's not that Gail spends too much, it's just that she's too emotional. Her moods fluctuate with how much money she has in her pocket. She doesn't see the big picture."

"MONEY ISN'T EVERYTHING, BUT IT'S BETTER THAN HAVING ONE'S HEALTH." —Woody Allen

According to a 1990 *Redbook* survey, money is the number-one reason couples argue.[3] Those benign green faces of our forefathers wind up causing the kind of discord that keeps psychologists and marriage counselors in business. Bizarrely, it seems that when there's more money, there's more tension. Couples who barely make enough between them to survive have fewer financial decisions to make. Most of the time their salaries are pooled together to make ends meet. But when there's a surplus, the complications begin. Whether it's due to her increased financial security and ability to make it on her own or her discontent with her marriage because of her career, a 1990 article in *Cosmopolitan* reported that every increase of $1,000 in a wife's earnings increases her chance of divorce by two percent.[4]

Dr. Jeffrey Lipner, a psychologist at the Nassau Center for Psychotherapy, says that, based on his experience working with Three-Career Couples, money is among the top three sources of marital discord (along with kids and sex). He adds that while partners think they're fighting over money, there's often an underlying question about who has more power in the marriage. "Traditionally, it's been men who would say, 'I earn the money; therefore I can make the financial decisions.' In recent years, as women are earning more money and making more decisions, men often feel a loss of power and control, which has led to an increase in marital disputes. In relationships where women throw their paycheck into the pot and allow their husbands to continue to make financial decisions, arguments over money seem less frequent."

"When we first opened our practice, we never fought about money because there was none left over," says Ellen, 43, a veterinarian in partnership with her husband Howie, 41. "But now that our practice is successful and we're doing well, annoying money issues constantly crop up and cause a lot of tension. If we have a surplus of a few hundred dollars after we pay our bills, we wind up fighting over what to do with it. What we imagined would be so much fun—earning more money than we need—has turned out to be a real problem. Howie always wants to spend it, but I'd rather put it into the bank. He yells at me that I don't know how to live for today, that I'm going to be one of those old ladies who leaves a million dollars to her cats. I bark back that he's an irresponsible child who never deals with the possibility of emergencies or sudden illness. Was life simpler when we had less? I'm beginning to think so."

When it comes to money, couples argue about *how* to spend it, *when* to spend it (buy now, save later; or save now so we *can* buy later?) or who should decide how and when to spend it.

When financial circumstances suddenly change, parts of us, previously submerged, reveal themselves. Audrey and Bruce, both 29-year-old teachers, learned this when they received an unexpected windfall. "I never imagined that an inheritance would cause such problems between us," says Audrey. "But when Bruce's aunt died and left him $40,000, we suddenly started to have fights about money for the first time. Before all of the money we earned was "ours" in one joint account, and we made money decisions together like a team. But Bruce became very possessive about his inheritance and was reluctant to call it "ours." It took almost two weeks of pondering and sighing (while the strain between us was unbearable) until we put the money into a joint bank account. But the fun wasn't over. Then we had to decide what we would do with it—should we invest it? spend part of it? use it as a down payment for a house? It seemed that our whole lives were consumed with that stupid money! Finally we compromised and agreed to open a six-month CD at our savings bank. At least we borrowed some time until we had to start fighting about it again!"

Sometimes money is a scapegoat—blamed for choices couples make that have nothing to do with financial considerations. "For months we were arguing about whether to buy a house," says Fran, 30, and the manager of a bookstore. "Doug insisted that we couldn't afford the expense. I disagreed and showed him in painstaking detail with bank statements, tax returns and future projections that we could. Then one day I overheard him talking to a friend about his fears that if he gave in to me our carefree days would be over, that soon we would feel the next logical step would be to fill it with kids, that our pickup vacations would become a memory the day we closed on a house. I realized that he wasn't really talking about money; it was more his vision of our life that was on the line."

When it comes to working through money issues, communication skills are equally as important as budgeting skills, says Judith Beckman, a certified financial planner, registered investment adviser, licensed stockbroker and president of Financial Solutions, in Westbury, New York. Financial issues that need to be clearly understood between partners include:

1) Will there be "his" and "her" money?

2) Will there be separate or joint bank accounts? If savings are possible, will there be "his" and "hers" savings, or "theirs"?

3) How will it be decided where the money is spent? Will

partners be accountable to each other for what they spend individually?

4) Will finances be managed on a daily, weekly or monthly basis? through an allowance? a team budget? a more creative plan?

5) If the second income is less than the first, how will it be used? for basic expenses? to be saved? for splurge money?

Money management should be a team decision. Among the alternatives for Three-Career Couples are:

1) The "Let's Pool It All Together" plan. Partners combine their total incomes and pay for everything jointly. This seems to be more popular among couples who marry earlier. They launch their partnership with hopes, dreams, empty bank accounts and no notion of dividing up their salaries.

2) The "Proportional Contribution" plan. Partners pool a proportion of their salaries for Third-Career expenses and keep the balance in separate individual accounts.

3) The "Equal Contribution" plan. Similar to #2, but partners agree on a specified amount to be pooled and each contributes equally, regardless of their salaries.

4) The "Pool Almost Everything" plan. An offshoot of #1 where salaries are merged into one account, except for a small designated amount of pin money that's set aside for each partner to spend as he or she chooses.[5]

5) The "Patchwork" plan. Partners have a number of different accounts for different purposes and decide together whose salaries go for which accounts. One of the most important accounts a couple can have, according to Ms. Beckman, is a "God forbid" fund, with enough money set aside to exist for between three and six months in case of emergency.

Once a plan is chosen, it doesn't mean that it has to be set in stone. Partners should periodically reevaluate their decisions. Important changes in life—the beginning of a family, a new job, a significant salary raise, an inheritance—may warrant modifications or revisions in the game plan. According to Ms. Beckman, couples are less likely to feel tension over money if they are willing to

1) listen to each other's needs;

2) set goals together and work toward those common goals;

3) negotiate issues and compromise to reach a mutually acceptable agreement; and

4) remember that there is not just one right way to handle financial issues—what works for one couple may be inappropriate for another.

WHO PAYS THE BILLS?

"Who pays for what, when, is never a one-answer issue," says Judy Beckman. "Sometimes the spouse with the higher salary will pay the mortgage and utilities, and the one earning the lesser sum pays for food, clothing and extras. Sometimes one partner enjoys the detail work and pays for everything out of a joint checking account. Each person might have his or her own savings account to assure a little cash for frills, gifts and surprises—but each should be well informed about the family's financial health."

"Neither of us particularly likes being in charge of paying the bills," says Leslie, the dentist who splits the workweek with her husband Art, a psychologist. "My nature is to worry about money, most of the time more than I have to. The one who pays, knows how dire the financial situation is at any given moment. We both take turns handling the checkbook till the other one has had it. When it's Art's turn, I try to stay as unaware as I can about whether there's enough money to paint the house in the spring or take a two-week vacation. This year for my birthday he relieved me of my fiscal responsibilities six months early. It was one of the best presents he could have given me."

Bill-paying options are clear. You can

1) have the more organized, more financially efficient person be in charge;

2) do it together, tackling bill paying as a joint project once a month;

3) rotate the position, with either clearly defined deadlines (switch every April 15) or when it stops being fun; or

4) hire someone else to do it. If you can handle a stranger being privy to your financial records, you can afford it and you both hate the task, this is a great idea.

"I've always dreaded Thursday nights, the time I set aside for the past ten years for paying bills," says Rhoda, a 33-year-old interior designer. "Bill would do it if I asked, but he's so lax about deadlines and so sloppy in his record keeping that I couldn't bear putting our financial reputation in his hands. A client of mine suggested hiring a bookkeeper. At first I thought it would cost too much, then that there wasn't enough for someone to do, then that I couldn't trust someone I didn't know. But I hated doing this job more than I worried about these drawbacks. I can't tell you what a blessing Roseann is. She comes every two weeks, picks up the checkbook and the unopened pile of bills I keep in a basket in the kitchen and pays them. She's neat, thorough, and the whole thing costs about the same as a weekly manicure. It might sound indulgent, but hiring a bookkeeper was one of the best things I've ever done."

It's Only Money

- According to the 1992 Hilton Time Values Survey based on interviews with 1,010 adults from across the country, Americans want to spend more time with family, but 53 percent still place increased importance on career advancement and 61 percent on making money.[6]

- The 57 million women in the United States work force, according to the Institute for Women's Policy Research, now earn 71 cents for every dollar earned by men. They make up over 45 percent of the labor force and will fill about 60 percent of the new jobs between now and the year 2000.[7]

- When asked by the General Social Survey conducted by the National Opinion Research Center at the University of Chicago, "If you were suddenly wealthy, would you keep working?" almost 75 percent of the men and 65 percent of the women said yes.[8]

- A 1990 Gallup poll found baby boomers increasingly pessimistic about their financial future. Thirty-one percent of those aged 30 to 35 and 27 percent of those 36 to 41 reported that they were not satisfied at all with their financial situation.[9]

- Money was cited third, behind accomplishment and achievement, as the best thing about work.[10]

A FINANCIAL PLANNER CAN HELP YOU GET YOUR MONEY ACT TOGETHER

"We always considered ourselves organized people," admits Barry, 32, and co-owner of a local deli with his wife, Sheila. "But we were always concentrating on trying to make money rather than planning how to manage it. We meant to make a financial plan for ourselves and our future, but somehow we never got around to it. Our immediate expenses like the mortgage, heat and phone bills took precedence every month, and then we had to pay for the kids' orthodontists and for new gutters and leaders or a new washing machine—there was always something that needed to be taken care of right then. College and retirement seemed so far away that we kept putting long-term planning on the back burner. But last year, when we had to pay so much in taxes that our vacation fund was drained, we realized we were doing something wrong and it was time to get some professional advice. We met with a financial planner who reviewed our taxes and our loans, talked with us about our future goals and helped us develop a long-range plan that even took into account projected college expenses for the year 2010."

Like Barry and Sheila, many of us are capable and competent at our jobs—but shaky on realistic budgeting, uncomfortable with financial planning and inexperienced at long-term investing. Just as we would seek medical advice from a doctor and legal advice from a lawyer, so too can financial advice be sought from a professional financial planner.

According to Judy Beckman, Sheila and Barry are among the majority in putting their emphasis on making money rather than on managing it in order to increase it. The result of failing to create a carefully thought-out plan of action is haphazard investing, which just doesn't work. Ms. Beckman explains, "You should be analyzing your investments in terms of which ones best suit your future needs, how they relate to the tax consequences of your income and how they are affected by the current economic realities. If you need to save for your first home, accumulate money for your children's future college education or build a fund for financially secure retirement years—and you're unsure of how to do it on your own—you probably need the services of a financial planner."

A financial planner is trained to design individually tailored short- and long-term financial plans of action for clients. This includes plans for asset management, taxes, retirement, savings, emergency funds, tuition, estates and family budgets. Getting your financial act together is not something you should do casually. It's up to you to find someone who you believe can provide realistic, understanding answers and who will continue to help you make the most of every cent you have.

Choosing a Financial Planner

Of course you know that there's not just one right person to assist you in making financial decisions. But following are some guidelines to finding a financial planner who can help you feel comfortable and confident:

- Look for someone who speaks your language—who can simplify concepts so that you understand them.
- Interview several experts. Get recommendations from friends and from your other professional advisers. Ask people whose financial goals and abilities seem about the same as yours.
- You can also contact either the Institute of Certified Financial Planners (7600 East Eastman, #301, Denver, Colorado 80231), which publishes a membership directory, or the International Association for Financial Planning (2 Concourse Parkway #800, Atlanta, Georgia 30328) for the names of local members who are certified financial planners or chartered financial consultants. Make certain you get answers to the following questions:

  1) What is the financial planner's training and background?
  2) What kinds of licenses and registration does the planner have?
  3) How long has the individual been practicing?
  4) What is the planner's specialty? Is it investments, insur-

ance, tax planning, retirement planning or something else? You want a planner with a wide field of expertise, but you also should want to know if his or her area of specialization matches your priorities.

5) Will the planning process include a written plan stating an investment strategy based on your particular needs?

6) Will the planner review the plan with you on a regular basis?

7) How does the financial planner charge for services? Some planners charge hourly or flat fees, some receive commissions and some charge hourly or flat fees for consulting and creating the written plan and also receive commissions generated by implementing the investment portion of the plan.

8) Will the planner provide you with the names of clients you could contact for references?

9) At what time is the planner available to meet with you? Will he or she be available when you are, or will you have to conform to his or her schedule? (For instance, can he or she meet with you in the evening or during the weekend if necessary?)

Only after you do your homework can you make a smart decision in choosing a financial planner.

———————

"After our second child was born, Bill and I decided to hire a financial planner," says Carol, 34, and an editor. "Afterward, we were very glad that we did. Right from the start she made us feel comfortable. A week after our two-hour meeting with her she gave us a detailed plan that took into account our current and projected future expenses, including our children's college needs. Since that evening we've kept an ongoing relationship with her and feel free to call her with our questions and concerns about money matters. She's advised us on investments but has never pushed. Only recently did we feel ready to invest some of our money with her, and she made us feel confident with our decision. For our personal financial plan drawn up six years ago, Bill and I paid about $600, and it was money well spent."

HOW MUCH OF THAT SECOND SALARY DO YOU REALLY GET TO KEEP?

If you knew back when you were still in school how much money two people living together would be grossing a year at this point, would you have thought it was enough? Enough to afford better housing, fancier cars, vacations, more savings and even good old elusive financial peace of mind? Probably. Till concepts like "real" dollars and taxes creep into the picture. Till you figure in the cost of clothes, transportation, fast food and child care. Till you grow up to realize working couples don't get to keep all that they make.

In fact, according to a 1989 report in the *Nation's Business,* a two-income family has these additional expenses over a one-income family:

- $1,500 to $5,000 a year on transportation (the cost of a second car, gas, repairs and insurance)
- $800 to $3,000 a year for clothing (depending on what your job is and what your taste is)
- $2,000 to $6,000 a year—or even more—on child care (with measly tax credit)
- up to $5,000 a year on miscellaneous costs (eating out, dry cleaning, paying for chores like housecleaning and yard work that there's no longer time to do)[11]

In a report in the *Journal of Marriage and the Family,* Sandra Hanson, Ph.D., and Theodora Ooms wrote that the payoff of two salaries actually diminishes as household income rises because affluent families spend proportionately more on work-related expenses like the ones mentioned above. Those who benefit the most from two sets of wages are low-income families. Middle-income families gain only 17 percent from having two of its members in the work force, and upper-income families net only 5 percent more than they would if just one spouse worked.[12]

But Work Does More Than Pay the Bills

■ Even if that second salary barely pays for more than the expenses it incurs, you have to consider that it's an investment for the rest of your life. The road to larger paychecks, promotions and greater job satisfaction starts here.

■ How much bleaker would life be without your contributions toward savings and down payments and family vacations?

■ What would your life be like five years from now if you stopped working today? There is more to working than making money. We work to become, not just to acquire. We work to contribute, to be challenged, to learn, to succeed. And as Shakespeare said, "If all the year were playing holidays, to sport would be as tedious as to work."

The expense that hits all working couples hardest is taxes. Because the tax law lumps the second salary on top of the first, federal taxes wind up with a sizable share of that second income. In a March 1989 report in the *Nation's Business,* it was written, "Chances are only the first salary will be taxed at 15 and 28 percent tax rates, and then, if it is large enough, at the 33 percent rate, while the second salary—when added to the first—may be taxed entirely at 33 percent. In such a case, if that salary amounts to $30,000, the Internal Revenue Service will get $10,000."[13] On top of that chunk come other deductions that make the second paycheck look mighty small indeed. In fact, the median-income ($53,984) family-of-four household spends 39.7 percent of its income on federal, state and local taxes.[14]

BRIGHTER NEWS FOR THE TWO-PAYCHECK COUPLE

While for the Three-Career Couple one-plus-one often equals less-than-two, there are money-saving plans and tax breaks that make it possible for you to keep more of that second income. For instance, tax-advantaged retirement savings plans allow your savings to grow untaxed until you withdraw the money and reduce your taxable income by the amount contributed to the plans. If the terms Keogh, IRA and 401(k) are unfamiliar to you, get acquainted with them now—they may become your greatest financial allies.

Here are some of your best money-saving options:

- An Individual Retirement Account (IRA) is a personal savings-for-retirement plan—your own private pension fund. The money you put in an IRA fund grows through years of earning interest to give you a high yield in your retirement. It belongs to you completely and can't be lost through any change in job, pension or marital status. IRAs enable two-income partners to each contribute $2,000 every year—thereby reducing their taxable income by $4,000 and deferring taxes on those earnings. The "but" to this benefit is a restriction added by the Tax Reform Act of 1986 that allows you to claim the deduction only if you are not covered by a pension plan or you jointly earn less than $40,000. (If your income as a couple is between $40,000 and $50,000, a partial deduction is allowed.)[15]

- For people who are self-employed or who have freelance income, a Keogh plan, much like an IRA, allows you to contribute 25 percent of your total self-employed earnings, or up to $30,000 a year. You can be eligible for a Keogh even if you also earn a salary, so long as you earn some outside income as a self-employed person. Like an IRA, a Keogh is a tax-deferred plan and an effective way to save for the future.[16]

■ The 401(k) is an employment-related retirement savings program managed by the company for which you work. As an employee you make contributions that are deducted from your payroll check, and your employer matches some or all of your contributions. There is a preset annual maximum contribution you can make—for 1993 it is $8,937. The benefit of a 401(k) is that your contributions are tax-exempt, and if your company is like most, it kicks in extra dollars. The entire account is tax-deferred until withdrawal.

To participate, you must first decide what percentage of your salary you want deducted. You have the option of changing your investments several times a year, and help is often available from financial planners who work with company employers. If you leave your job, your 401(k) plan must be rolled over into an IRA or into a plan connected with your new employer within 60 days to avoid any penalties.[17]

■ A tax-deferred annuity can function much like an IRA. You pay a premium and your interest will be tax deferred until payout. (In most tax-deferred plans, you must be age 59½ to receive your payout without a penalty.) Unlike IRAs there is no maximum deposit, but tax-deferred annuities are not tax deductible. (In other words, you cannot deduct that part of your income that you invest in such an annuity.)[18]

■ When filing tax returns, if one spouse in a Three-Career Couple has large business or medical expenses, your tax bill may be reduced by filing separately. In order to qualify to write off these costs, your miscellaneous business expenses must exceed 2 percent of your adjusted gross income and your medical bills must be greater than 7.5 percent of that income. By filing separately, the spouse with the high expenses may have a low enough income to qualify for the deduction.[19]

■ There is also great potential for savings in health insurance options. If you are lucky enough to work for a company that offers a flexible benefits plan (one that allows you to choose from a variety of coverage alternatives the one that best fits your lifestyle), you and your spouse can maximize on savings. For instance, if you are eligible for coverage under your spouse's plan, you may be able to decline medical coverage and net an extra $50 to $75 a month in your paycheck. Or you might elect the "working spouse option," which makes your employer liable for 20 percent of your reimbursable medical expenses and relies on your spouse's plan to pick up the rest. The savings offered by the various options depend on the way the plans are designed. To decide which is the most cost-effective policy, weigh the price of the options against the cost of your coverage under your spouse's plan (and your spouse's coverage under yours).[20]

Admittedly, the changing tax laws often seem confusing and options in savings plans can be overwhelming. That's why there are professional tax advisers and financial planners to help you make the best decisions, both for now and for the future.

PAYING THE SITTER—
TAX CREDIT MAY SPELL RELIEF

A chapter on finances wouldn't be complete without discussing child care—often the largest expense for parents of preschool children. We spend years saving for our children's future, but major expenses actually begin before the kids even learn to talk. A 1989 report by *Money* magazine estimated that the annual bills for child care range from $1,500 to $10,000 a year, with the majority of parents paying about $3,000.[21]

The good news is that there is some tax relief for working parents. In addition to the exemption you can claim on your tax return for dependents (up to $2,150 per child), you may also be eligible for tax credit for 20 to 30 percent of your day care bills. The credit—a dollar-for-dollar reduction of your tax bill—can save you as much as $720 for one child and $1,440 for more than one child. To claim child care credit:

- expenses must be for the care of a dependent under age 13 for whom an exemption can be claimed
- claimant must live with the child
- claimant must have earned income during the year
- child care expenses must be work related[22]

The other way parents can recover some child care costs is through employer-sponsored flexible spending accounts, which many—but far from all—companies offer. Employees put up to $5,000 taxfree, pretax dollars of their annual salaries into the account earmarked for child care expenses. Families in higher tax brackets can save about $2,000 in federal and state taxes.

Check with an accountant to make sure you take full advantage of benefits that are rightfully yours.

EVEN FOR DINKS, THE BUCK STOPS HERE

For the 4.2 million married couples whose dual income is free of the expenses of raising children, life is full of financial possibilities. Discounting those who are just biding their time till the babies come (they don't count because they should be in a saving mode from day one), DINKS (dual income, no kids) have a discretionary income that's enviable. It gives them the luxury of making their dreams of retiring or opening their own business come true.

There is a danger, however, in trading a future of station wagons and trips to Disney World for a life that promises less limited funds. No matter how you decide to spend your money, you still have to accept financial responsibility for your later years. Money management, fiscal planning and mature restraint are concepts that apply to all of us, no matter how many members there are in our family.

"Sometimes I'm embarrassed by how much we used to spend," says Elliot, 42, an assistant district attorney. "I don't use cash as much anymore because my money would disappear without a trace. It was irresponsible, I know, but those ATMs became an extension of my wallet. Now I write more checks and use my charge cards so I have a record of exactly where all the money is going. When I saw how much Donna and I spent on eating out, I was amazed. It's not that we don't go out as often now—it's just that not all of the places have three-star reviews. Donna has this thing about shoes—jokingly we've come to call our spare bedroom 'the shoe room.' It wasn't that funny, though, when we totaled up what she spent in six months. She still loves shoes, but now restricts her buying to those she absolutely must have."

There's no reason DINKS can't save 15 percent of their gross income, says financial planner Judy Beckman. "Many have lofty goals they'll never attain unless they discipline themselves to live on less. For those who find saving too painful, I recommend automatic payroll deduction savings plans that invest in choices like U.S. savings bonds, and I suggest balancing that with allocating money to growth funds—conservative or aggressive, depending on the couple's comfort zone. If they can participate in a profit-sharing or a 401(k) plan, they may find saving money easier than doing it on their own. It becomes like paying a utility bill or a car payment."

Taxes can be harsh for two-income couples with no dependent care deductions to reduce their income. It's not uncommon for federal, state and local taxes to take a bite of a third or more of whatever's earned. Here again 401(k) plans and health care reimbursement accounts, funded with pretax dollars, can save you a great deal. In a 1989 article, "The Rewards of Being a DINK," in *Money* magazine, Jeanne Reid wrote, "For instance, if you are in the 28 percent bracket and contribute the maximum $7,627 allowed in your 401(k) this year, you would shave $2,135 off your tax bill. As a bonus, most employers will throw in 25 cents to $1 for every dollar you put in, up to 5 or 6 percent of your income. In addition, the money accrued from the investments grows taxfree until you withdraw it."[23]

WOMEN AND MONEY—BECOMING GOOD FRIENDS

"When I was growing up, my father was in charge of all financial matters," says Ilene, 32, a children's librarian. "My mom never knew how much money they saved; she didn't have a clue about their investments or what insurance coverage they had. When my dad died suddenly she was a basket case. I swore I'd never be so uninformed. Even though talk of municipal bonds and mutual funds makes me break out in hives, I don't run away. I can say I'm an educated investor, and that feels great."

Like Ilene's mother, many women are uncomfortable in the world of finances, says Shelley Freeman, director of personal financial planning at Shearson Lehman Brothers, a subsidiary of American Express, in New York City. "For some women, fear of finance comes from never having been taught about managing money by their parents. This is compounded by an industry that has largely ignored women. Finally, women have let the industry, and the people in it, ignore them; they have not taken enough responsibility for educating themselves about finances. But times are changing, and women are hungry for financial knowledge. We see evidence of this in the multiplying number of women who fill seminars on investing and financial planning."

Surprisingly, says Ms. Freeman, younger women (in their twenties, thirties and forties) are less knowledgeable and less sophisticated about investing than are more mature women. Why? "There is no data to help us analyze these observations," she says. "One theory is that older women are more willing to take risks because they feel they have less to lose. Another possibility is that older women have accrued more money and therefore have more interest in learning about investment options."

A 1992 study by Shearson Lehman Brothers, reported by Ms. Freeman, compared men and women investors with at least $20,000 to invest. The results were interesting:

- There were no significant differences between men and women in their attitudes about security and retirement.
- The major difference between men and women was in terms of risk. Women identify themselves as being more conservative than men do. When asked if the kinds of investments they buy would be considered conservative, moderate or aggressive, conservative was the choice of 81 percent of the women compared with 71 percent of the men.
- Women are more likely than men to stay with an investment decision once they make it, despite its ups and downs.
- Women are more likely than men to rely on the advice of a financial adviser. "My guess," says Ms. Freeman, "is not that women are less educated about money than men, but that they are more willing to admit when they're lost."

Consider also the following statistics, provided by Prudential Bache securities:

- 75 percent of all married women outlive their husbands
- 53 percent of individually held stock is held by women
- 86 percent of the personal wealth in America is controlled by women[24]
- Women now play an active role in deciding what to do with their money, and investment companies that once dealt pri-

marily with the man of the family have shifted their attention to include both partners.

SUMMING IT UP

Money. The same money that Joel Grey sang about in *Cabaret* as making the world go round can be both a source of pleasure ("I got my bonus—it's vacation time!") and anxiety ("Bad year—no profits, no vacation"); power ("*I've* got the money!") and greed ("I want it!"); fulfilled dreams ("If we can just save $100 from each paycheck for the next five years, we'll have enough for the down payment on that cute little bungalow") and marital tension ("What do you mean we can't afford a new car for me—*yours* isn't ten years old!").

Whether we make money, spend money, save money, waste money, invest money, lose money, argue over money or worry over money, financial issues surround our lives. As the new Three-Career Couple you're likely to feel more in control over the Almighty Dollar if you:

- Take charge of your finances. Become—and stay—informed and educated. Familiarize yourself with investment options and savings plans like Keoghs, IRAs and 401(k)s. Take advantage of tax deductions and deferrals. Do everything possible to become best equipped to make responsible financial decisions.

- Form a partnership plan for money management. Include a plan for paying the bills that falls within the comfort zone of both spouses. Your plan should not be considered a "forever" decision, but one that will need reassessment when there is a major change in your lives or if one partner begins to feel dissatisfied with the arrangement.

- Work as a team in exploring needs, discussing financial goals and looking for answers concerning your future together. Teamwork includes short-term planning (making a realistic budget) and longer-term planning (a five-year plan—maybe even ten).

- Keep in check with the real world. This begins with a practical perspective on the worth of money (it doesn't measure your value as a person, it only brings you goods and services). It also means watching your credit cards and charge accounts, paying bills on time and making up a budget and savings plan with a cushion.

- Consult a financial adviser on any issues with which you are uncomfortable or uncertain—from child care tax credits and investment options to life insurance, health insurance and disability insurance. Recognize the importance of addressing these critical financial issues. When needed, ask for assistance from a trained professional who can guide you wisely in budgeting for today and in investing for tomorrow.

HONEY, HOW WOULD YOU LIKE TO LIVE IN DES MOINES?
Impact of Career Choices on Family

What you have become is the price you paid
to get what you used to want.

Mignon McLaughlin

It's hard to imagine that as recently as 1977, 60 percent of the female population agreed that supporting a husband's career was more important than for the wife to have one herself. Fifty-two percent of the men surveyed thought they were right. Only twelve years later these numbers were cut drastically, when only 29 percent of the females and 27 percent of the males still believed in this sacrificial truth.[1] Talk about a revolution. For better or for worse, the two-breadwinner family has changed the way we all look at work.

More of today's husbands realize they don't have to climb the work ladder—if they choose not to—in order to support their families. More than 50 percent of 500 men questioned by Robert Half International, Inc., an executive recruiting firm in the finance field, said they would be willing to cut their salaries by as much as 25 percent to have more family and personal time.[2] A study of workers at two federal agencies in Washington, D.C., showed that 47 percent of fathers opted to change their schedules when offered more flexible hours.[3] Employees are beginning to refuse transfers for family reasons. Companies have been forced to find new ways to move people up without moving them around. Huge businesses like Xerox, Mobil and General Motors are experimenting with moving jobs rather then transferring people, and they are cutting professional development stints overseas to six months, down from two to three years.[4]

According to a 1990 poll published in the *Wall Street Journal,* 59 percent of human resource executives think that the availability of a flexible schedule will be a highly important recruitment feature in the future.[5] Those numbers are complemented by a study cited in She Said, He Said, a 1992 compilation of polls conducted by the University of Chicago's National Opinion Research Center, of 521 personnel chiefs who give their overwhelming endorsement to such work options as part-time employment, job sharing and flextime.

Most of us were raised in families where Daddy decided what was best for his career and whatever that was—a move, longer hours, more schooling—the family went along. The only thing considered was his well-being in the workplace; raises and promotions took precedence over the rest of the family's concerns. Change had to happen if his boss willed it. Today, making such career decisions can be a lot more complicated because often there are two jobs involved.

"I met Jody in our second year in medical school," says Jon, a 29-year-old internist, now married to Gwen. "We went out for over a year and probably would've stayed together if it weren't for our careers. I got a residency in Boston; she got one in St. Louis. Neither of us was willing to compromise—or carry on a two-year long-distance romance. We both realized how important it was to wind up where it was best for our professional lives. If the person we chose to share life with couldn't be flexible enough to follow us anywhere, it would never work. We both ended up marrying accountants. Luckily they pick up and travel more easily."

While women have always been aware that their careers are part of a larger whole, many men have been raised to see success in life solely in terms of success in the office. But in what we believe is a life-affirming change for the better, a good percentage of these men are broadening their definition of the good life.

"Now I praise myself not for how many hours I put in and how many late and early meetings I attend," says Les, 34, and a managing partner in a New York law firm, "but for how I've arranged my schedule to drive Katie to school or for how many nights I'm home by six. I was the first guy in my office to take advantage of a two-week unpaid paternity leave. My firm never publicized the fact that paternity leaves were allowed—even though they were. They preferred negotiating time off on a case-by-case basis, making you ask for what you're entitled to. When I got back, I expected to be viewed as less committed. I even dreamed about a group of guys lined up in my office trying out my chair. The truth is, my fears of being stigmatized were much greater than the reality. And if I'm perceived by some as not being as interested in going to evening functions and taking clients out for dinner, what can I say—they're right."

"Les is lucky," says his wife, Julie, a 35-year-old social worker. "He can afford to integrate what he wants to do with what he has to do. A lot of men aren't in that situation. It took me a year of constantly thanking him for 'helping,' for being available, for coming home early if I had to work late before I realized he was doing this for himself, not for me. He wants more from his life than long hours, high pressure and no family time. I'm sure some of his coworkers aren't happy with his attitude, but he'd rather satisfy us than them."

As long as men continue to earn more than their wives do, career decisions by most families will be made giving men more latitude.[8] In 1989, about one third of all working women were secretaries, teachers, semiskilled machine operators, managers and administrators, retail and personal sales workers, and bookkeepers and accounting clerks. These jobs are easier to leave and reenter. Their educational requirements aren't as rigorous, and this type of work allows women more time at home to fulfill other responsibilities.[9]

But times are finally changing, albeit slowly. As women assume more responsibility in the workplace, their strengths are being acknowledged. Although today more opportunities for women are found in smaller organizations than in large corporations, their cooperative style of leadership, different from men's "command and control" relationships, is proving effective and successful. Judy Rosener, a professor in the Graduate School of Management at the University of California at Irvine, has done research showing the style of women as one that "encourages participation, shares power and information, enhances other people's self-worth and gets others excited about their work."[10] With women investing more in their educational preparation and being offered greater opportunities to prove they can handle more responsible positions, we optimistically look forward to the day when men's earnings are no longer used as the yardstick to measure women's, and women's earnings are no longer described as a percentage of men's.

DECISIONS, DECISIONS: WHAT IF...

Changing life patterns as a result of women's empowerment have been described by Felice Schwartz, the author who ignited the "mommy track" debate. In her latest book, *Breaking with Tradition,* she tells us that:

- Fifty-two percent of all undergraduate diplomas are awarded to women.
- Of all master's degrees awarded in 1989, 51 percent went to women—up from 31.6 percent in 1960.
- Women earned 2.6 percent of MBA's in 1965—and 33.6 percent in 1990.
- Women earned 5.5 percent of master's degrees in accounting in 1965—and 43.7 percent in 1990.
- Law degrees rose for women from 2.5 percent in 1960 to 40.8 percent in 1990.[11]

Add to that the findings of a 1992 report by the Women's Bureau of the U.S. Department of Labor that reveal women accounted for a substantial share of master's degree confirmations: 79 percent in health sciences, 74 percent in education, 25 percent in physical science and 13 percent in engineering.[12]

According to Ms. Schwartz, women's success in school sets them up for equal acceptance in the workplace and positions them to surge ahead in fields that have been traditionally male dominated. Like it or not, changes are forcing many Three-Career Couples to address these career "what if's":

1) What if a career decision benefits one partner but is not in the best interests of the other—or the family?

2) What if one partner has a "golden opportunity" that hinges on relocating?

3) What if one partner's career goals can only be fulfilled by going back to school?

4) What if career advancement means having to sacrifice family and leisure time?

5) What if each partner has a different—and conflicting—definition of success?

Such questions don't come with a manual to answer them. Under the best circumstances, fitting two careers into one marriage is a challenge. According to Ellen Galinsky, copresident of The Families and Work Institute, in the past, career decisions were made predominantly by the spouse who earned the most money. While this is still true in many families, an awareness of how these decisions affect the entire family is growing. More and more the bottom line is: If there's resentment within the family, then the decision just won't be worth it.

Three-Career Couples can work as a decision-making team by:

1) Examining the pluses and the minuses—both short term and long term. "What does this change mean for us today? Five years from now?"

2) Evaluating expectations. "What will life be like if we agree to your working more hours?" "What pleasures will you give up in your decreased leisure time—watching football? coaching Little League? me?" "Will I have to start walking the dog because you're not around?"

3) Negotiating and compromising. "I'll give Omaha a try if you agree that if I'm miserable after one year, we can come home." "If I decide not to take this job to give us more time to spend together, I need to know that you will compromise on your hours also and not work till 9:00, three nights a week."

4) Involving the kids. "How do you feel about going to a new school? We know change can be tough. What can we do to make it easier for you?" "Each of us is going to make sacrifices while Mommy's in law school. What can you do to help us out?"

WHEN CAREER ADVANCEMENT MEANS A MOVE

"When Paul burst into the kitchen carrying a bottle of champagne and, with the biggest grin, announced, 'Honey, guess what? We're moving to Ann Arbor!' I nearly fell off my chair," says Helen. "He was so excited with the news that he just received an associate professorship at the University of Michigan, he didn't even notice my stricken expression."

"She's right, I was insensitive," admits Paul. "But this was my dream come true. I just assumed that Helen would be as thrilled as I was. Besides, I knew she wasn't attached to her copywriting job in Boston—she always complained about the dull assignments and lack of stimulation in her office. And the kids were still young. If there was ever a right time to move, we were facing it."

"I couldn't bring myself to talk to Paul that night," recalls Helen. "I was too emotional, too angry with the way he sprung this on me, as if what we did with our lives was his decision alone. The next morning we sat down and discussed it, as my parents would say, like two adults. Everything Paul said was true. The kids were four and six at the time, still flexible and adaptable. I wouldn't have any regrets leaving my job, and with my experience, finding another writing job in a city like Ann Arbor shouldn't be too difficult. As we talked, I got excited about all of the positive aspects of making the move. By that evening, we were *both* ready for that champagne!"

According to a 1990 report in *Time* magazine, while women are still the trailing spouse in 94 percent of job transfers that involve couples, the numbers are changing rapidly. By the end of the decade, almost a quarter of all transfers are expected to be women.[13]

Easing Relocation Pains

New job, new city—as easy as 1-2-3? Not! The emotional and economic complications involved in relocating are forcing companies to take note. Slowly, they are beginning to respond.

- In 1990, of the 1,000 companies that belong to the Employee Relocation Council, based in Washington, D.C., 75 percent offered services designed to make relocation more attractive to spouses. Services ranged from writing resumes and pooling job listings with other companies to expediting a spouse's employment search.[14]

- Career Relocation Corporation of America, based in Westchester County, New York, is one of several companies offering career counseling to spouses of corporate transferees. The company contracts with certified career counselors in more than 150 locations throughout the country. Executive Vice President Harvey Mills says that today 30 percent of American companies offer spousal assistance.

- Burroughs Wellcome Co., a manufacturer of pharmaceuticals in North Carolina, started a relocation policy in 1985. For entry-level employees, the policy provides for a five-day house-hunting trip, temporary living expenses and moving costs. Benefits for mid-level and experienced employees also include closing costs on the purchase of a new home and the option to have the company buy their old home at 100 percent of its appraisal value. For top-level employees, add to that a discount on the purchase of a new home and an allowance of $3,000, or five percent, of their annual salary. In 1989, 162 employees took advantage of relocation benefits, and, according to Pat Smith, relocation manager, the policy has increased the rate of acceptance of new-employee job offers and has generated positive feelings about the company.

- In 1987, Dow Chemical U.S.A. implemented a dual-career assistance program. This was established as a benefit to Dow employees who were offered transfer opportunities within the company and for prospective employees with working spouses as an aid in recruitment. There's a network of dual-career coordinators located at each of Dow's major company sites in the United States. Coordinators work with the trailing spouse to find local employment opportunities and assist them with resume writing, interview techniques and career counseling, if appropriate. The program focuses on information and training to help in the job search. In its first year, the program serviced 147 people, with a placement rate of 85 percent.[15]

For Three-Career Couples, the decision of whether to relocate should include:

- a job comparison—whose job pays more money? Whose job gives greater personal satisfaction? (In 1987–89, 47 percent of the men and 44 percent of the women surveyed said they loved—really loved—their jobs.)[16] Whose job has more opportunity for advancement? Who is more willing to change?

- an assessment of other factors, including kids, location, housing market, commuting time and social opportunities.

Once a team decision is reached, partners should periodically reevaluate their choices. As life changes, so, too, may their decisions.

For Peter and Ann, both in their late twenties, an unexpected move to Santa Barbara was the consequence of an offer too perfect to refuse. "We were always New York people and never thought about living in California," says Peter, a sculptor. "But when Ann's boss asked her to run their gallery's new West

Coast showroom, we suddenly started thinking sunshine and palm trees. I could set up my studio anywhere, and what could be more inspiring than working while overlooking the Pacific Ocean?"

For Fran and Roger, however, a company job transfer to Chicago, offered with a sizable raise and bonus, was unanimously vetoed. "When I came home with the news, the whole family freaked out on me," recalls Roger, 47, and a sales manager for an electronics company. "Our kids were both in high school—probably the worst possible time to ever think about moving. Fran was recently promoted from assistant art director to head art director in the advertising agency, and she wasn't ready to give that up so fast. I was a little disappointed to turn down such a good deal, but it was either that or being excommunicated from my family. So New Jersey, here I stay."

WHEN THE GOING GETS TOUGH, EVERYBODY STARTS SWEATING

When career decisions cause a two-career collision, it's time to take action! Following are the stories of three couples who faced difficult choices and found successful solutions.

"Timing is everything," Debbie, 33, reflects, looking back on turning down an enticing job offer. "We had been married for a few months when the position of my dreams fell out of the sky. At any other time of my life I would have jumped at the chance to be the buyer for one of the most prestigious accessory shops in Boca Raton. It made my job—working on the floor in a department store—look pretty dismal. But my experience in retail told me the job entailed a lot of traveling. I didn't think that would be fair to Burt—or our new marriage. A week in New York and a week in L.A. every month would never allow us the opportunity for intimacy we had both been looking forward to. Burt was so smart. He offered no help in this situation;

he waited patiently—and silently—for me to make the decision on my own."

"Your turn, my turn" is the agreement that allowed Joanne and Todd, both 36, to each fulfill their personal goals. "When we got married ten years ago, I was in law school and Joanne's teaching salary paid the bills," says Todd. "She also had wanted to go to law school, but that was financially impossible. So we made a deal. Joanne continued teaching during the years I finished school, took the bar exam and set up a practice. Now that the kids are seven and four, it's Joanne's turn. She started law school last year, and I've rearranged my hours to carpool the kids and make dinner four nights a week. It's not easy for either of us, but there's something noble about being half of a true partnership."

A new definition of success was written into Alan and Terry's dictionary when they agreed to sacrifice a higher salary for more time with each other and their daughter. "It was basically a quality-of-life decision," says Alan, a 40-year-old accountant. "Terry owns a delicacy shop that's open late two nights and weekends. I was with a Big Eight firm and worked till ten every night but Friday, when I'd get my first chance all week to see Lindsay before she went to sleep. We brought home great paychecks but were always either too tired or too preoccupied to enjoy them. Finally one night about six months ago we sat down and talked about how little fun we were having.

"All of a sudden it became clear that we were totally responsible for putting ourselves in this predicament and totally capable of finding a solution. The next week Terry hired an assistant to cover for her on Thursday night and on Sunday. I found a new job with a small company where it's not a sin to walk out the door at six. Our family income has shrunk and the transition was a little bumpy, but at this point in our lives it was the right decision."

THE NEW SUCCESS—MAKE ROOM, WEBSTER

Like Alan and Terry, many Three-Career Couples have begun to redefine success. Have you? Would you consider yourself successful if you

    A. made $150,000 a year, were well-known and respected in your field and saw your spouse and kids only on weekends and holidays?

    B. loved your job but barely made ends meet?

    C. both of the above?

    D. none of the above?

Ellen Galinsky says, "In a series of focus groups run by The Families and Work Institute, we asked people to define success. Success at home was most often defined in terms of everyday moments—coming home at the end of a hard day to find relief with your kids, being able to make it to the soccer game, finding a few minutes to read a bedtime story. Responses to success at work were interesting. Words most often used included flexibility and control. Yet we are seeing many contradictions. While people crave flexibility and control in their jobs, they hesitate to take advantage of alternative work arrangements for fear their careers would be jeopardized."

In a 1989 survey of women attorneys, cited by author Felice Schwartz in *Breaking with Tradition,* 90 percent said they believed that even if their firm offered part-time or flexible work schedules, women who used those arrangements would be slowed or blocked in their quest for partnership. "Women are disillusioned," Ms. Schwartz says. "They look at the generation just ahead of them and recognize that they can't 'have it all.' They realize much more clearly than men that 'all' includes real involvement in family life, and they don't want to settle for "'either or.'"[17]

A 1992 study called Money and Making It was conducted by the Roper Organization for Shearson Lehman Brothers, a division of American Express specializing in investment research. The results are revealing. When asked to evaluate their careers in terms of personal versus financial rewards, the majority of respondents said that job satisfaction for them is more personal than financial. Twenty-one percent of the men and only 15 percent of the women said they got both personal and financial rewards from their jobs.

According to the study, people most likely to find their careers more personally rewarding include:

- college graduates
- those between the ages of 55 and 64
- executive professionals

People most likely to find their careers more financially rewarding include:

- those between the ages of 30 and 39
- those with household incomes over $100,000
- blue collar workers

And those most likely to choose a different career if they could largely belong to the "thirtysomething" generation.[18]

"We're in a period where the old think and the new think are coming in at the same time," says Ms. Galinsky. "There's an ambiguity—between greater demands in the workplace and the desire for more family and leisure time."

PART-TIME, FLEXTIME OR WHAT TIME?

If you mentioned to your grandmother that your company had instituted a flextime policy, she'd look at you funny and shrug her shoulders, probably not knowing what you're talking about. Terms like job sharing, flexiplace and telecommuting would also leave her bewildered. But for today's Three-Career Couple these concepts are not so unfamiliar, and for many they are attractive alternative work arrangements.

A 1992 survey of 427 human resource executives conducted by the Olsten Corporation, a New York-based provider of temporary personnel, found alternative scheduling strategies for employees gaining widespread use in the workplace.[19] But a 1991 study released by the Families and Work Institute rated corporate America just mediocre when it came to helping its employees balance work and family life. On its report card it gave large United States corporations a *C,* with a *B* for effort for their establishment of work-family programs in response to employees' needs.[20] And while more companies are adopting credos of "family friendliness," many are finding that it's largely a piecemeal effort.[21]

Most companies agree that accommodating working parents is important. Yet how to do it is a matter of increasing debate. Studies consistently show that flexible arrangements have a positive effect on workers' attitudes:

- In a national survey on flexible time, an analysis of 92 organizations found that alternative work schedules reduced absenteeism and tardiness, and over a long time span reduced turnover.[22]

- According to a 1991 report in *Fortune* magazine, professionals who have flexible work arrangements are fiercely loyal to their employers and strive to prove themselves worthy of their company's trust.[23]

- Companies like U.S. West Telecommunications, Inc. report a savings of $4,000 to $21,000 annually for every telecommuter—measured in terms of office space saved, absenteeism prevented and retention of workers who might otherwise leave the company.[24]

Yet, as more and more flexible work arrangements are being requested, tested and touted as truly making a difference, workplaces in which employees are evaluated by performance rather than presence and praised for getting the job done whenever and however they choose, are for many still the ideal. And while 88 percent of large employers offer part-time work and 77 percent offer flextime,[25] many employees are still afraid that asking for these options can be the kiss of death.[26]

The programs most widely available to help families balance job and family life include:

- Flextime programs. You want to get to work at ten o'clock in the morning so that you have time to get the kids off to preschool—and you're able to stay at work until seven o'clock at night because your spouse is home by four o'clock in the afternoon? No problem, as long as you accumulate the prescribed number of hours each week.

Sounds great, but a majority of flextime programs have been implemented on an informal basis and are not available to all employees. Among companies surveyed by the Corporate Reference Guide, reported usage of flextime programs is less than 10 percent, and it is used predominantly by clerical support staff.[27]

- Voluntary reduced time. It's not a permanent situation, but for 6 to 12 months, if you need to be home more and work less, it's now possible. You'll take a pay cut, but you'll retain your benefits and seniority status.

- Flexiplace (work-at-home). According to the Olsten survey, this is the fastest-growing type of alternative arrangement. More than 10 percent of companies now have employees working out of their homes, telecommuting via computers. Half of these companies report an increase in the number of home-based employees.[28] Under certain conditions, employees who care for children or elders can benefit from flexiplace arrangements, although parents of small children will most likely still need child care support while working at home. It is typically professionals who participate in flexiplace programs.[29]

"Working at home is not for everybody," says Pat, an editor for a women's magazine. "But in my case, it's been the key to my survival. Thankfully, I have an employer who has supported my decision to work four days at home, one in the office. It's still full time—actually I work longer hours when I'm home because I don't have to spend time commuting and I don't watch the clock. If I'm in the middle of a project and the house is calm, I keep working."

"I try to ensure that calm by hiring a high school student to supervise the kids when they get home from school. I didn't do that for the first three months of this arrangement, falling into the trap of thinking that if I'm home, I must be available to my children. The truth is, my body is home but my mind is at work. The day I saw that clearly was the day my professional life really fell into place. In return for getting to stay in jeans and a T-shirt, I have to overcome the loneliness and fight sometimes to stay focused. On Friday I'm in the office, and I get to put on a suit and attend to necessary meetings."

"Being able to take a half hour break at 3 p.m. four days a week to greet my kids, have a snack and find out what's going on in the first and second grades are the best reasons for choosing this arrangement."

- Part-time work. Part-timers have traditionally been treated like the stepchildren of the American labor force. But now, according to the *Corporate Reference Guide to Work-Family Programs,* nearly nine out of ten companies provide some benefits to their part-time workers. Half either extend full-time benefit protection to part-timers or prorate these benefits according to the number of hours worked. Like other alternative work arrangements, part-time schedules are primarily a white-collar prerogative and apply largely to the clerical and sales fields.[30]

- Job sharing. Love your job, but can't give it the hours it demands? By splitting one job with a compatible partner, you can work less and enjoy more. In its classic definition, job sharing refers to two workers who divide the responsibilities and benefits of one full-time job. While job-sharing programs were found in 48 percent of the companies surveyed by the Families and Work Institute, formal policies and companywide availability were rare. Still a relatively new concept, there are pluses and minuses to this arrangement.

On the positive side

—You work less than full time.

—The flexibility of hours can often be worked out with your partner.

—Shared jobs are often more interesting and responsible than those usually offered to part-timers.

—Working with and learning from another person can be very stimulating.

Jobs can be shared by friends, strangers or spouses. An arrangement between husband and wife, if the family can afford to live on one income, allows partners to stretch their professional horizons, spend more time with their children and make less use of outside child care. Admittedly, this type of arrangement is rare, but if it works, it really works.

On the down side

—It's less pay than full-time work.

—There are fewer fringe benefits than those that come with a full-time job.

—Personal performance may become blurred in the team effort, putting a sharer at a disadvantage in terms of salary and advancement.

—The closeness of the relationship may give rise to competition and personality conflicts.

—Job requirements and jurisdiction may be ambiguous, leaving partners unsure of their exact responsibilities.[31]

I'M LEAVING ON A JET PLANE...AGAIN

The U.S. Travel Data Center reports that out of the almost 20 percent of people that travel for business, 62.1 percent are married and nearly 43 percent have children. Although about two thirds are men, the number of business trips taken by women increased from 47 million to 54 million between 1987 and 1989. The average time away from home, said to be four nights per trip, leaves millions of neglected chores, missed birthdays, unattended school plays and unanswered calls for help on the home front every day.[32] Few people think business trips are glamorous after the first one or two, yet the perception still is that being away is more "fun" than being left home.

"I hate leaving home so often," says Barry, 40, co-owner of an alarm company and the father of three. "My business keeps me on the road six to eight days a month. Thank God for camcorders or I'd never have seen my son score the winning goal in the soccer championship or my daughter blow out the candles on her fifth birthday. I call home every day when I'm away, but Jane is usually too frazzled to really talk and the children are curt because they're angry that I'm not there. Lately I've started to send postcards to each of them when I'm away. I know how they love to get mail. We have a big map of the U.S in the den and they find where I am and put pushpins in that city. It helps them feel connected to me and makes it easier to picture how far away I really am."

"It's murder being married to someone who travels so much," says his wife, Jane, 32, and a nursery school teacher. "As much as I know he'd rather stay home, as sure as I am that he's tired and lonely, it's hard not to see him having an easier time of it than I do. We try to make the separation more bearable by leaving little notes for each other. I slip one into his attache case; he leaves mine under the pillow. He sends flowers often—sometimes to me, sometimes to the kids—just to say he misses us. The day he comes back is exciting, but it's never worth how depressed I am the day before he leaves."

ANYTHING YOU CAN DO, I CAN DO...IF I WANT TO

On the home front

As the structure of our home life changed from a complementary, clear division of labor where one partner (most often the husband) called the shots to a more equal sharing of all responsibilities where the division of territory and related tasks is blurred, entitlements are healthier and no one's needs automatically take priority, the issue of who gets to sit down and read the newspaper after dinner becomes tougher to resolve.

According to Dr. Arthur Mones, a New York family therapist on the faculty of St. John's University and the Family Therapy Training Program of the Long Island Institute for Psychoanalysis, the problem of competition at home between partners in a dual-career family is a real one. It begins with divvying up two different levels of responsibility: One, the "executive" level, on which tasks are planned and overseen (remembering birthdays, keeping in mind the dwindling pantry supply, updating the children's car pool schedule); and two, the "hands-on" level, on which chores are actually carried out (buying presents and sending gifts, shopping for food, chauffeuring the children).

The executive level, if lodged mostly on the shoulders of one spouse, can place that person in a managerial position, orchestrating the activities of the rest of the family. On the other side, if a spouse is mostly called upon to be the hands-on person, he or she can feel overburdened and uncomfortable in a childlike, subordinate family role. Very often a husband or wife will absorb both executive and hands-on levels of responsibility, resulting in one form or another of psychological stress.

On the work front

There are certain times when the difficulties surrounding matters of competition are greatest. They can occur when:

- one partner is at a low point in his career, while the other is achieving success.

- one partner becomes less available because of added work responsibilities and the other has to take up the slack.

- one partner experiences sudden and unanticipated success and his or her behavior changes.[33]

Deciding whose work takes precedence is one of the hardest problems any Three-Career Couple can face. Feelings of injustice, self-sacrifice and jealousy may all be involved. It's hard to be rational—or honest—about these emotions because their roots are found deep in family histories of sibling rivalry and in one's concerns about self-worth. The relationship's basic structure is exposed as partners are forced to confront the answers to these questions:

- How willing am I to compromise my needs for the sake of a shared future?

- How seriously do I take my spouse's work?

- Is how much each of us earns the only criterion for whose work is more important?[34]

Partners can protect themselves from the "slings and arrows" of a loved one's jealousy by learning to enjoy his or her own successes. It's a fantasy to believe that your spouse will always be able to share completely and equally in each of your triumphs; what's prime time for you might be the worst time for your partner.

"You must put other things aside," says Dr. Mones, "and make working out these problems about competition a priority. Because these behaviors have roots that go way back, they take time and patience to change. Sometimes it's hard to know if the difficulty comes from the marriage itself or from a more personal source."

Dr. Harold Lief, professor emeritus of psychiatry at the University of Pennsylvania School of Medicine in Philadelphia, writes in *Redbook:* "Sometimes when people are able to carry on a dual-career marriage, it enhances the relationship enormously because they can share each other's work experiences. There is the potential for what is called a 'total' relationship. What we have to avoid is the tendency to measure the prestige, financial success and rewards of one partner against the other."[35] Keep in mind that competitions are for horses and athletes—not husbands and wives.

SUMMING IT UP

Life in the days of the one-breadwinner family was indeed simpler. There were fewer conflicts over career decisions, fewer commuter marriages, fewer "quality of life" discussions about juggling and balancing success and fulfillment. Life now for the two-breadwinner family brings with it new definitions of success, opportunities, rewards and advancement, and a multitude of decisions.

While nobody is promising easy answers, you as a new Three-Career Couple will be better prepared to face the decisions of Detroit versus Des Moines, full time versus flextime and career advancement versus leisurely weekends, if you:

- analyze career decisions together—what they will mean for you today and tomorrow. If you base these decisions purely on money, be prepared to have to earn it in more ways than one.

- communicate your concerns and expectations for yourselves and for each other. Each of you answers to a different set of demands without benefit of rehearsal or respite. Since so much of life is based on how your partner assesses the job you're doing, give each other the time and consideration you both deserve.

■ listen to your partner with an open mind and a willingness to compromise. The days and months and years consist of a series of mid-course corrections. No mistake need be final. Be flexible and forgiving.

■ cooperate as a team to set priorities and goals, and then to develop a game plan to achieve them together. Marriage has been called our last best chance to grow up. Prove it true.

CHAPTER 9

I MISS YOU; FAX ME A HUG
Making Time for Each Other

*Love is the ideal thing, marriage a real thing, a confusion of the real
with the ideal never goes unpunished.*

Goethe

Read the personal ads. Then you'll remember the reasons you chose your spouse. Here was someone committed to complete, intuitive understanding of your every mood. Each of you would bring equal measures of generosity, respect, encouragement, fidelity, harmony, laughter and passion to the relationship. Then marriage came along and structured the demands of your relationship. When the pressures of parenthood were added to the equation, it seemed that the only thing left of your courtship was a memory and the only pleasure shared equally was a ten o'clock bedtime.

"It's just no fun anymore," moans a generation of Three-Career Couples, as the protector, provider and procreator reveals his fragile ego, and the tender, loving nurturer is too wiped out to care. Spouses give each other the dregs of their lives, talking with each other as little as 15 minutes a day, mostly about logistics and money, house matters and child care. Exhaustion leads to apathy, and any smidgen of quality time is spent on kids, extended family and friends. Couples stumble through the day, then come home to collapse. Yet according to any poll you pick up, married people are happier than single people—even when they're wretched.

Sociologist Andrew Greely, in his book *Faithful Attraction,* reported that a 1989 Gallup poll found that four out of five people would marry the same person again if given the chance.[1] This, even though 56 percent of the women and 55 percent of the men in a 1990 *Time* magazine poll felt it's more difficult to have a good marriage today than it used to be.[2] According to the *Journal of Marriage and Family*'s Index of Marital Success, 49.9 percent of those married three to five years and 33.3 percent of those married nine to eleven years said their marriages are "very happy."[3]

In the overprogrammed 90s, even happy marriages sometimes have their share of communication glitches and thinly disguised pleas for attention. Have any of these exchanges become familiar refrains in your home?

- "Nothing new ever happens around here."
- "You call that a hug?"
- "Why don't you tell me what's on your mind?"
- "I may not be looking at you, but I am listening."
- "It's been *how long* since we've made love?"
- "Please put down the paper. I want to talk to you!"
- "What exactly do you want from me!?"
- "You talk more to your friends than you do to me."

- "You pay more attention to the kids than you do to me."
- "You'll never understand what my life is like."
- "Your work is more important to you than mine is to me and I hate it."
- "I do love you—I'm just too tired to show you how much."

IF I'M NUMBER ONE, WHY DO I FEEL I ALWAYS COME LAST?

"The biggest problem we face is having no time alone together," says Gerry, 34, a computer salesman and father of an eight-month-old daughter. "We have no patience at the end of the day to express how we're feeling the way we know we should. Instead of being careful to say things in ways that won't hurt each other, we just spew whatever's on our minds. The serious issues and decisions we really need to make we avoid because we don't have the energy to deal with them. Too much of the time we scream at each other first, then backtrack to the root of what's really bothering us. I guess it's normal to take advantage of the one you love the most because you think that person's a sure thing and you're not afraid of losing him or her. It's sad though, and I wish there were a better way."

"The most bizarre example of how bogged down we get in this life happened to us last summer," says Arthur, the psychologist we met in Chapter 4, who splits his workweek with his wife Leslie, a dentist. "Lara was in camp four weeks before we realized that we didn't have to alternate our days off. Here was an opportunity for us to work the same days and enjoy our time off together—and neither of us realized it for four weeks. How ridiculous."

Probably the greatest loss to most Three-Career Couples is making time together a priority. Chances are that if you exercise or belong to a book club or are a member of a social or professional organization, you'll find the time to incorporate those things into your life. But time alone often gets forfeited until an alarm goes off. Usually it's the wife who becomes disenchanted first with the lack of intimacy.

It's no secret that men tend to be better at figuring out spatial and abstract relationships and women excel at verbal expression and the ability to understand emotions. It's difficult for some husbands to comprehend thought processes built on something other than logical, concrete information. They are baffled by some of the indirect methods of showing dissatisfaction that their wives use. Likewise, because each gender employs its own socialization skills and communication style, women have little tolerance for talking to a husband who's watching TV or one who sets aside problems in the hope they can be resolved with little or no attention.

Pop psychology books have bombarded the market with tales of how a woman's need to communicate on an intimate level is much greater than a man's. They describe how women engage in deep, direct eye contact conversations with their friends and miss experiencing the same type of sharing with their partners. Men's friendships, because they tend to be centered around the sharing of activities and possessions rather than personal feelings, are more distant and removed.

Communication for boys is a means of negotiating status, challenging others and establishing who's up and who's down. Girls use language as a way of establishing connections and closeness.[4] But no matter how much we read about our differences (boys being biologically directed to high action, aggression and confrontation activities versus girls centering on caring, loving, tenderness and relationships), the fact remains that as schedules tighten and undercurrents of tension rise, the need to stay in touch with each other's feelings increases and the opportunity to do so decreases. Lots of us are locked into schedules that allow for little latitude.

What's most important is the belief that the relationship between husband and wife be one of the primary things in which both partners are interested. If you can't *find* more time right now but the commitment to *create* more time together in the future is there, your relationship will remain strong. Trust and closeness can be fostered just as easily discussing joint involvement in family and household maintenance as it can be in discussing Ibsen and Matisse. Doing grocery shopping together on a weeknight or spending Sunday together cooking some of next week's meals can, when other options aren't viable, redirect a partnership that is growing distant.

I HEAR YOU, BUT I'M NOT LISTENING

"I was daydreaming, vaguely hearing Donna's voice in the background," recalls Phil, the pediatrician introduced in Chapter 2. "She was telling me about a matrimonial case she just won, and I'm embarrassed to say I hadn't heard a word. When she stopped her story in midsentence and asked me if this was how I listened to my patients, I snapped to attention."

"I know he's tired at the end of a day," says Donna. "We both are. At work we're both on all the time; we give our patients and clients the best parts of us—undivided attention and never-ending understanding. But does that mean there's only so much good stuff inside and there's less left for each other?"

Many of the skills that assure success on the job can also be used in your marriage, says Dr. Sally Ridgeway, professor of sociology at Adelphi University. The same attention and respect paid to people at work should be employed at home:

- If you can organize your schedule at work to set aside an hour for a business meeting, why not an hour to meet your spouse for lunch?

- If you can plan an advertising campaign from start to finish, what about planning a weekend getaway for two?

■ If you can discuss problems and explore solutions with your coworkers, isn't it as important to do the same with your spouse?

■ If you can delegate unimportant tasks at work to avoid work overload, why feel that you have to do everything yourself at home—especially when it takes time away from being together?

Bringing the goodwill, enthusiasm and effort from the workplace home with you is bound to improve your personal life. But not *all* business skills are best brought home. A competitive spirit that works well on the job should be left there. At home partners should not see each other as adversaries but as friends cooperating on the same team.

"Donna's jarring question forced me to realize what I was doing—what we were both doing," says Phil, "We were so focused on our work that we started to take each other for granted at home. Luckily this is one of those problems that started to resolve itself once the awareness kicked in."

GIVING IN INSTEAD OF GIVING UP

When you finally do find the time to be together and your interests don't coincide, it's insane to waste an hour arguing over whether to eat Indian or Japanese, to see Woody Allen or Steven Segal. Giving in and compromising are the only ways to go.

"Hope wanted to celebrate our anniversary with a trip to France," says Larry, a 42-year-old dentist. "I hate long plane rides, rich food and being in a country where I don't know the language, but I said okay. While I have no burning desire to go back there, it wasn't as bad as I thought. The next month I became president of my university's dental alumni scholarship fund. Hope, who's a professional fund-raiser, took a busman's holiday and coordinated a campaign that made me look amazing. She might've helped if we didn't go to France—but not as generously. We sincerely got as much pleasure making each other happy as we did being the recipient of the other's kindness."

"Jay is a sports fanatic," says Marcy, 39. "He has season tickets to the Knicks, and because he's in the limousine business and made some influential friends he gets tickets to the Superbowl every year. I can tolerate basketball and football, but they're far from my favorite things. As much as I try to convince him to take a friend to the Superbowl who would so much better appreciate the whole event, he really wants me there. So I bring my knitting and I go. It's a small sacrifice, really, and he's so grateful that I wind up having a good time just watching him."

I SAID "ONE NO TRUMP"!

"Brian and I thought that the best way to guarantee us time together would be to engage in activities as a couple: take courses, learn to ski—you know, broaden our horizons as a team," explains Ellen, 30, a hairstylist. "The trick was to find something that interested both of us. First we looked through our local adult ed catalog. We settled on duplicate bridge. That was our first mistake. I had played a little bridge in college but didn't remember very much. Brian, on the other hand, thought he was an expert and had a sarcastic comment for every card I played. Week after week I left every class with a headache and a knot in my stomach. After six sessions I admitted defeat. We would have been better off staying home and watching TV."

Shared activities can bring a couple closer—if interests are not forced. Doing things together is important, but not as critical as sharing common values and goals. If couples get involved in a competitive activity—like bridge or tennis, for example—it can create marital conflict and be more of a detriment than a help to their relationship. When seeking togetherness, it's a lot safer to choose noncompetitive activities.

Ah, but when it works...

"We love to have fun together," says Adele, 45, a data processor. "Over the past 15 years we've taken painting lessons together, courses in Chinese and Italian cooking, workshops in yoga and transcendental meditation and wine tasting seminars. Some have been a bust—like the painting—but each new experience has brought us closer. Whatever course we take or activity we do is built-in time together and gives us something to talk about and look forward to (or dread) as a team. Last spring we took up golf, and every Tuesday during the summer we both left work a half hour early and played nine holes before the sun went down. It was our time: two hours alone, away from everything and everybody."

STOP THE MERRY-GO-ROUND; I WANNA GET OFF!

"We've gotten so used to the merry-go-round we're on that we rarely stop to think about how fast we're going," admits Bernie, the husband who recently learned how to make pasta in Chapter 4. "I walk in from work, Jane rushes out to her exercise class; she sets aside an evening to play with the baby, I'm stuck at a late meeting. It went beyond being dizzy, however, last month on Jane's thirtieth birthday when I worked so hard to plan a surprise celebration that would be especially meaningful for her. It was a surprise all right—to me—when she said she couldn't go out that night. I knew Jane's job was important to her, but never before did I feel like I took second place. And as if that wasn't a big enough disaster, she wound up totally annoyed with me because I got so upset!"

"Bernie overreacted," explains Jane. "Don't get me wrong; I thought his idea was wonderfully sweet and thoughtful, but he knows how erratic my work schedule is. He should have checked with me first to make sure I was available that evening.

It wasn't that I didn't appreciate his gesture—I just had no choice. I was the one giving up my birthday celebration. I just couldn't believe how personally he took all of this...."

The trick to finding time together is planning ahead for it, keeping lines of communication open and being especially sensitive at all times to each other's work requirements. Dr. Ridgeway explains that in many cases scheduling issues underlie other power struggles. Who is defining the relationship? Who is defining time and how it is spent? Who is defining priorities? Jane's guilt about not being seen as an appreciative wife led her to become defensive and angry, while Bernie thought he'd be adored and rewarded for being so nurturing. If partners can sit down and talk through these issues, they can learn to better understand themselves, each other and whether their expectations of their marriage are realistic.

"For months Mark and I were on opposite schedules with very little common time," confesses Anya, 40 and a librarian. We never had time to talk, no less relax and enjoy each other. Finally we called an SOS to my parents, and they came to stay with the kids while we escaped to a hotel in the mountains for two days. When I returned to work Monday morning, four different people complimented me on how relaxed and energized I looked. The best comment was from a colleague who said, 'I don't know what happened to you, but all the hard edges are gone.'"

HELP! CURE ME OF MY KIDITIS!

Were the most recent conversations you had with your spouse about philosophy? psychology? politics? *Or* were they about where to send Jamie to nursery school, when to start toilet training Joey and how to discipline Jennifer?

Were your last few dinners at home peaceful and relaxing—conducive for sharing thoughts, feelings and the details of the day? *Or* were they accompanied by a toddler throwing food from his high chair, by one child yelling at a second who was busy making faces at the third?

Did you spend your last few weekends at an old film festival watching *Casablanca*? sitting in a dark corner at a romantic table for two? taking a long walk followed by a leisurely cup of cappuccino at a cafe? *Or* were you on the soccer field passing out orange juice and cheering for Jason, buying new sneakers for Michael and having Julie's ears pierced?

If your responses fell where we think they did, chances are that you are, at this moment, suffering from "kiditis": the acute need to spend some time with your spouse away from the kids. If you can't spare a week, and you'll settle for a few hours, here are a few suggestions.

"Whoever named the terrible two's, didn't yet get to four," says Joanne a 33-year-old teacher. "Four-year-old Nicki is the center of our universe, but she's so totally demanding that Paul and I can't even carry on a conversation with her in the room. By the time she falls asleep at night, we crash right after her. Romance? It's buried somewhere under the Legos and the Play-doh.

"Each week we faced the same long seven days, until my neighbor and I came up with our Saturday night kid-swapping plan. Each couple gets one free 24-hour period each month. On our weekend off, Doris picks Nicki up Saturday about noon, and Paul and I go out shopping or to a movie. We have a lei-surely dinner together, then the entire night to ourselves, with no interruptions. We even get to sleep late on Sunday morning, have breakfast in bed and relax with the newspapers. That 24 hours feels like a B12 shot!"

Kids are often the best form of birth control, says Dr. Jeffrey Lipner, a psychologist at the Nassau Center for Psychotherapy. Too much togetherness with no relief can lead parents to resent their own children. Periodic breaks from the kids for a long weekend or even a few hours are healthy—and necessary.

"We needed a break but had no one to watch the kids," admits Amy, a 31-year-old physical therapist and mother of two preschoolers. "Don and I were on total overload. We each had a few vacation days coming but no game plan. Finally we decided that getting away with the kids was better than not getting away at all. Then we discovered a resort hotel with a day camp program for the kids. They were thrilled to be involved in arts and crafts, gymnastics and indoor games, and we were ecstatic to have our own time to go horseback riding, play tennis and escape up to our room for a siesta. By the end of the day when camp was over, we were all ready for a family reunion."

For Rosemary and David, both 35 and English teachers, a periodic break from their four kids (ages two to ten) is a must. Facing the challenge of a tight budget and the need for time alone, they started a tradition of a date every Friday night. "We make the most of our schedules as teachers," explains David. "One of the perks is being finished with the workweek by three o'clock on a Friday, and we begin our date then."

"First we tried staying nearby—going to an early dinner at a neighborhood restaurant or to a local movie. But that wasn't relaxing. We were always interrupted by people we knew, and if our friends had their children with them, we felt guilty that we left ours at home. So we formed our '20-mile plan.' Every week we look through the papers for activities—art fairs, foreign film festivals, stuff like that—and every Friday we head for a different destination 20 miles away. We use the time in the car to unwind, listen to our music and catch up. Nothing we choose to do is expensive, so our biggest expense is paying for the babysitter."

ROMANCE IS A STATE OF MIND

Not everyone has the need to travel 20 miles to spark the romance in their relationship. For Margie and Dan, the best times together are right in their own home.

"Our favorite part of the week is Sunday morning when both kids are in Sunday school," says Dan, 39, an architect. "We put on the answering machine and hide away for two hours. Our lovemaking is never as relaxed—or playful. Bagels and coffee in a quiet kitchen are a treat. Feeling like we're sneaking makes it even better. That time is set in stone in our schedule, and aside from religious holidays and the flu, nothing has ever interfered with it."

Romance is a state of mind, says Dr. Lipner. "It can be created cheaply and easily anywhere, by willing partners who know what works for each other. Complaints of 'not enough time' and 'not enough money' are just poor excuses."

"We grab an hour here, an hour there—whenever we can," says Janie, a 31-year-old interior designer and mother of six-year-old twins. "With the twins, the easiest place to grab time together is at home. It's not that we're sex maniacs, but Vic and I do like our private time to snuggle and talk, and, yes, make love. Now that the girls are a little older, they can occupy their time for an hour or so—especially if equipped with a good video and a few snacks.

"So at opportune times—Friday evening, Saturday morning, whenever—we get them settled and make a game out of our escape. After they watch their movie, they have a short list of easy chores to do on their own like putting the newspapers in a bag for recycling, feeding the cat and watering the plants. We give them a timer set for a half hour after the video is over, with instructions to come get us when the timer goes off—not before—unless it's an emergency. If they last till the timer sounds, they're rewarded by very grateful parents. (And eight out of ten times they do.)"

EARLY TO BED...

We know that sex is fun. We know it's free, has no fat or cholesterol and is readily available. If only we had the oomph, the time and the motivation to enjoy it. Masters and Johnson's latest book, *Human Sexuality,* states that "the average American married couple in their twenties and thirties has intercourse two or three times a week, after which the frequency slowly declines."[5] According to the couples we interviewed, numbers like these put more pressure on an area that needs anything but more competition to get where it should be.

In 1990, *Esquire* magazine reported that after raising their wives' self-confidence, the things husbands would change next about them would be their sexual attitudes (31 percent) and their sexual performance (20 percent).[6]

"In the last few months, every time I initiated lovemaking I felt like I was pushing a hot fudge sundae on someone who's just eaten a five-course meal," says Scott, 29. "We've all been told the most powerful sex organ is the mind, but no matter how much we love each other, I can't empty Sheryll's mind of enough 'stuff' to make sure she concentrates on only me."

Helpful books like *The Crisis of the Working Mother* tell us that "the quality of our sex life is vital to the intimacy of our relationship. It affects how we feel about our partners and ourselves. Our sexual relations have the capacity to make us feel loved, accepted, attractive, powerful, giving, given to. Or they can make us feel the opposite—unloved, unwanted, rejected, unattractive, vulnerable."[7]

Many Three-Career Couples lose interest in sex. The fantasy of being wonderfully, overwhelmingly lost in merging with another, without regard for agenda or time, is exactly the opposite of how we've programmed ourselves to live the rest of our lives. Following are some ways the couples we interviewed thought of to put their sex lives in proper perspective:

"For a while we were hung up with the myth that good sex needs a lot of time. So rarely did we have that much time that our lovemaking really suffered. We have sex more often now that we give ourselves permission to count quickies as 'quality' sex."

"Just like I can't wait for inspiration to motivate me at work, I can't wait around for spontaneous and unplanned sex. If we don't make a date for sex, we don't make love. I used to think that these things would just happen normally and naturally, but life has been anything but normal and natural for years. It's no less romantic—in fact, now we have fires going and warm baths waiting. We leave messages in code on each other's machines, and since anticipation is now added to passion, our sex life is more rewarding than ever."

I used to think that locking the bedroom door and saying 'Daddy and I need some private time' was wrong, but now that the kids are eight and ten they're at an age to understand that we sometimes need to spend time alone without them. What better message could I send them than that their parents' relationship is strong and loving? They make breakfast on Saturday morning, giving us some extra time alone in bed. They know to knock before entering and respect us as a couple as well as Mommy and Daddy."

"Because our time together is so limited and fragmented, we both decided to play hooky. We took a day off from work, drove out to the beach, took a room overlooking the ocean and had the most romantic afternoon in years. We were home for dinner and no one ever knew. We vowed to incorporate more interludes like that into our lives. Priorities deserve the undivided attention needed to take care of them—and that afternoon reasserted the fact that we are our most important priority."

"It drove me crazy that these friends of ours were constantly bragging about how often they made love. Until they separated. Only then did I see that frequency is no measure of quality. For them, sex was more about needs and power than it was about love. Now with no one keeping score, we're both more relaxed."

CAN YOU SQUEEZE YOUR KISSES THROUGH THE PHONE WIRE?

If time together for the Three-Career Couple is scarce, it's at a premium for the almost one million American couples who work in different cities (sometimes different countries) and see each other only on weekends, or even less. According to the *Wall Street Journal,* international commuter marriages appear to be gaining in popularity, largely as a result of married women being less willing to give up their careers for their mates. Surprisingly, a 1992 study found in *Health* magazine reveals that of more than 200 people in long-distance relationships, couples who work in different cities feel no more stressed than dual-career couples who live in the same place.[8]

A clearer separation of work and family sometimes makes it easier for partners to handle multiple roles, explains Dr. Ridgeway. While live-at-home couples have to juggle everything at once, commuter couples can more easily focus on their careers and themselves during the week, and on each other and their Third Career on weekends. That's not to say that it's easy to stay connected. Being separated by miles can mean disrupted routines, lonely nights and many microwave dinners for one.

"Having a long-distance commuter marriage was never our first choice, but we couldn't see any other alternative," says Cindy, a 32-year-old New York stockbroker, married to Greg, 35, and a lobbyist who spends Monday through Friday in Washington, D.C. "When we made the decision to try this arrangement, we also decided to hold off having children, until—-and unless—our lifestyle changed. During the week Greg and I direct all our energies toward our work and ourselves. We speak to each other before going to bed each night, and we use our fax machines to send each other messages.

"We stick to a strict schedule on the weekends: Friday night and Sunday are ours alone—no intruders permitted. Saturday is for socializing, along with the agreement that there's to be no talk about work. The arrangement is not easy, but I think we make the best of it. I'm sure our friends wonder about our relationship, but thankfully, I don't think being a commuter couple has affected our marriage. If anything, because time is so precious, we appreciate each other even more."

THANKS FOR BEING MY BEST FRIEND

Falling in love is easy—it's staying in love that's the challenge. It's no secret that sustaining the romance in marriage takes continuous work. We know it's important to compliment each other, to recognize each other's accomplishments and triumphs, to please each other with little gifts for no special reason, to include each other in decisions, to stay in touch physically, emotionally and sexually. But too often, on a three-career merry-go-round, we forget to keep up with the simple things. That's why we could all use a periodic recharging— whether it's a week away in the Caribbean, a weekend tucked inside a romantic inn, a day of playing hooky together or a few hours hiding in the bedroom. Sometimes it's the smallest actions, the most fleeting moments, the silliest gestures, that help keep the love alive.

On their tenth anniversary, Marcia sent her husband, Bob, a card, on which she wrote: "For all the wonderful 'little things' you've done for me over these ten years that nobody knows about but me, I thank you. For

1) warming up my car on cold mornings while I gulp down a cup of coffee;

2) emptying the dishwasher because you know how much I hate to;

3) checking on my mother on the nights I'm out of town so she won't feel lonely;

4) saying thank you after every meal, whether it's something that's been cooked for hours or has been picked up from the deli;

5) calling every day before leaving work to ask if there's anything I need;

6) reminding me every day that you think I have the best smile in the world;

7) sneaking out of the office a little early on days I'm stuck staying late so the kids won't wait too long for both of us;

8) being as happy as I am when good things happen to me;

9) cursing the people I don't like; and

10) being my best friend.

For these, and everything else about you, I love you."

SUMMING IT UP

He walks in from work, she walks out to her exercise class. She falls into bed at eleven; he's already snoring. She rolls over to touch him the next morning at six; he's left for the office. He tries to tell her about his day; she's trying to pacify a screaming toddler. So go the woes of the Three-Career Couple.

We wish we could promise you an extra day in your weekend. Or that we would take your kids for a week and send you off to Paris. Instead, we hope that the examples in this chapter offer reassurance—that you're not alone; inspiration—that there's hope and that there're options to finding togetherness; and motivation—to take action. Bear in mind that for the new Three-Career Couple:

- It's essential to carve out time in your schedules and plan for togetherness.

- It's better than okay to make dates for sex.

- It's acceptable to teach your schoolage children that parents can lock their door and have some quiet, uninterrupted time together.

- It's important to stay connected. Use the telephone, fax machine, love notes—anything to let your partner know you're thinking of her or him.

- It doesn't take a reason to celebrate. If it's not your birthday or anniversary, maybe you lost five pounds, finished an assignment or even just made it to Friday night. Find a reason, stick a candle in a piece of cake and celebrate a few precious moments together.

CHAPTER 10

CAN'T I EVER PUT MYSELF FIRST?
Finding Time for Yourself

If you begin by sacrificing yourself to those you love, you will end by hating those to whom you have sacrificed yourself.
Self-sacrifice is suicide.

George Bernard Shaw

The thing about time is that when it's stolen, we don't notice it missing for quite a while. The thief, our hectic lifestyle, is masterful. It keeps us absorbed in the future, gives being productive more credence than it deserves and insinuates that we are legitimized more by what we do than who we are. Experts might congratulate us for having it all, but if all we can manage to do is acquire things, take care of them and read about ways to better deal with what we have, then maybe we'd better make time to reflect on what we *really* have in our lives.

A 1990 readers poll in the *Ladies Home Journal* found that the top family-related problem for mothers is finding time for themselves.[1] If there were a *Gentleman's Home Journal,* we're sure the results would be the same. Studies have shown that two-career parents spend as much time with their children as families in which only the fathers work, making up the difference on weekends. When mothers work, they seem to give what little time they have for themselves to their children—losing even more of their personal time.[2]

Are we so committed, so challenged, so controlled by the life we've mapped out that we leave the regulation of our internal thermostat to fate. With so many forces pulling at us, competing for our attention, it's difficult to carve out the time we need to laugh with friends, listen to music or engage in an activity without a shred of redeeming social or intellectual value. Unless we're sick or in pain we feel guilty attending to ourselves first. Yet the poster in the doctor's office reads, "Life is not a dress rehearsal." This is our one precious go-around on planet Earth, and there is no point in waiting for someone to hand us a permission slip to take time off and give ourselves a little pleasure.

A daily 15 minutes alone to renourish may do the trick for one, while somebody else might need a four-hour block of time on the weekend. Experts may differ on the optimum prescription for time-out, but all emphasize that the time needed varies with the individual. What's easier than figuring out how much time you need for yourself is recognizing when you're not getting enough of it.

In a 1992 article in *McCalls,* Judith Sills, a clinical psychologist, cautions that if you find yourself getting irritated at other people for no clear reason, what you may really need is more time for yourself. She says the three red flags are:

1) You've run out of empathy or sympathy for other people.

2) You find you cannot speak nicely to strangers—you see innate hostility in cab drivers, waiters and salespeople.

3) You feel the people close to you take more than they give.

Once you've recognized your "time-for-yourself crunch," the next step is to find that time.[3]

NEVER ALONE, NATURALLY

"The imagination needs long, inefficient, happy idling, dawdling, and puttering," writes Brenda Ueland in her book *If You Want to Write.* "These people who are always briskly doing something and are as busy as waltzing mice have little, sharp, staccato ideas, such as 'I see where I can make an annual cut of $3.47 in my meat budget.' But they have no slow, big ideas."

"Ideas come with the dreamy idleness that children have, an idleness when you walk alone for a long, long time or take a long, dreamy time at dressing or lie in bed at night and thoughts come and go, or when you dig in a garden or drive in a car for many hours alone or play the piano or sew or paint alone . . . that is creative idleness. At such times you are being slowly filled and recharged with warm imagination, with wonderful living thoughts."[4]

Denying ourselves this gift that only time alone can bring is the mistake of a lifetime. With only our thoughts as company, we have the opportunity to renew, rejuvenate and refocus the direction of our lives. Privacy is the necessary first step to get to healing solitude. And although it can be scary, the self confronting the self, it can also illuminate.

"My wife can't understand why I never complain about running to Dairy Barn for milk," says Dave, 26, an assistant editor. "I'd do almost anything that would give me time to be alone, time for me and my psyche to duke it out. Sometimes I take a walk around the neighborhood at night. I'm the only one walk-ing without a dog. Most of my friends walk or jog for exercise, and they all wear headphones. Not me. I walk to stop sweating, to stop my heart from racing. And I walk to be aware of what I'm thinking, not block it out with music or talk radio."

"I look forward to my Saturday list of errands," says Rob, 38, and owner of two doughnut shops. "I put on my 'so glad to be out of the house without the kids' demeanor and drift through the afternoon. I know it sounds strange, finding soul searching time in the mall or solitude in Home Depot, but I do. At this point in my life, that's the extent of my free time. It's time where my thoughts are not consumed with things I ought to and should and even could be doing—even if it's spent on a store check-out line."

Ten Thoughts on Why It's Important to Give Yourself Time Alone

1) Who deserves every sweet consideration you can eke out of this life more than you?

2) We all need to reintroduce ourselves to ourselves every so often.

3) How can you know if these are the best years of your life unless there's time to mull them over?

4) Big deal if you get the job done—if the job does you in.

5) Doing everything squeezes out any time to do nothing.

6) If you still feel lazy, guilty and worthless taking quiet time for yourself, you haven't taken enough.

7) Balance takes concentration; concentration needs quiet time.

8) If we adults do not affirm the worth of solitude, our chil-dren will never know they deserve *their* time alone.

9) Giving yourself time to be alone is not a luxury. It's a right and a necessity.

10) "Like water which can clearly mirror the sky and the trees only so long as its surface is undisturbed, the mind can only reflect the true image of the self when it is tranquil and wholly relaxed." —Indra Devi

---

YOU GOTTA HAVE FRIENDS

The complexity of our lives makes finding and keeping good friends harder than ever. Pursuing and maintaining close friendships takes the time and energy found in adolescence. So friendship, Three-Career Couple style, usually subsists on phone calls and letters, with only occasional glimpses of the magic chemistry that makes friends of strangers. When we asked our couples for the most recent nice thing a friend did for them, we came up with quite a diverse list. They tell us, "My friend:

- recommended a good book.
- sent the funniest card.
- got me to try Afghan food.
- told me my ex-boss went bankrupt.
- listened to me whine for an hour.
- picked up my kids from the library.
- lent me a car.
- made me laugh so hard with the same joke he's told me ten times before.
- gave me some clothes her kids outgrew.
- told me I looked thin.
- remembered the day my mother died.
- bought two tickets for us to go to a Rangers game.
- sent my business a new client.

■ showed up on time (for a change).

■ was ecstatic when I got a promotion.

■ understood why I had to cancel lunch for the third time in a row.

■ forgave me for forgetting his birthday.

■ taught me a new computer program.

■ convinced me to let go of some anger.

■ shared an investment tip.

■ filled me in on an episode of *Northern Exposure* that I had missed.

■ ignored my nasty mood.

■ trusted me with a secret.

Women are said to place greater importance on intimacy in friendships, whereas men's relationships are grounded more in competitive, work-related or social activity. Men tend to reserve intimacy for romantic relationships. Although they value their friends, men are reluctant to assign them the top value they might've in the past when they spent more time in the company of men. Many men will say that their best friend is their wife, while their wives will more likely answer that question with the name of another woman.

Three-Career Couples have only limited psychic energy to expend. Their schedules demand that they invest their emotional dollars wisely. Friendships, at this point, cannot be evaluated on the time spent together. True friendships are cherished in good times and appreciated even more when we're needy. Honest friends give the kind of unconditional support and pure acceptance found in perfect mothers. They enhance the rest of life.

"As lucky as we are to have friends in common, Eric and I are even more fortunate to have strong, stable friendships that precede our meeting each other," says Carrie, a 30-year-old advertising executive. "When Eric (who's a physician) is on call, so are my friends Jill and Sharon. They're single, they don't stand on ceremony; they feel as happy as I do when an unexpected opportunity to spend some time together comes up. Otherwise we grab breakfast twice a month and have a long phone conversation one night during the week. Eric sees his friends at lunchtime and Saturday morning on the basketball court. We come back to each other energized."

"We have so little time together," says Burt, the Florida restaurateur from Chapter 3, "that I feel guilty if I'm not spending my free time with Debbie. I never golf with the guys when she's home, but her work schedule gives me enough hours to get out and play. The only advantage of having different times off is the chance to do things with friends guiltfree."

"My friends are victims of my overly full calendar," says Shelly, 43 and a paralegal, married to Paul, 40 and a lawyer. "I'm doing what I swore I'd never do—making dinner appointments two to three weeks in advance. I start writing my Christmas letter in October to all our friends who live far away. It's strange about the friendships we've formed together—very few share our profession or our hobbies. In these relationships we talk mostly about kids and books and vacations we plan to take. They are just as valuable as the friends we grew up with, only we're less emotionally demanding of them. I assume that's maturity."

"My friends and I exchange gifts of self indulgence for any occasion we can think of—birthdays, anniversaries, stopping smoking, promotions, losing weight or just having the courage to tell off an abusive being," says Brenda a 37-year-old telemarketer. "For Christmas this year I gave my favorite thing: a gift certificate for a massage. Judy bought me a cosmetic makeover, Nan sent a gift certificate to a day spa and Jane gave out Godiva chocolates. Our history makes us aware of what will bring us pleasure. And giving, when you know it's really appreciated and well received, makes exchanging presents so rewarding. It's an old line, but it's true—friends are the family you choose."

ALL FREED UP AND NO PLACE TO GO?

By now you should be convinced that you deserve, are entitled to and need time for yourself. The next step requires incorporating leisure activities into your schedule and making them a regular part of your life. For some, the path is clear. If you're an exercise nut, a collector or a craftsperson, such activities may come easily. But if you've never longed to collect stamps, yearned to ice skate or sighed over the possibilities contained in a slab of clay, the choice of what to do with leisure time may not be so simple.

"I've always wanted to have a hobby," says Robin, a 37-year-old financial planner. "Everyone in my family has things they love to do. My husband plays basketball, my kids collect baseball cards, my mother knits. So last year I decided to try gardening. I bought dozens of packets of vegetable and flower seeds and set aside a little area on the side of the house. After two weeks of feigning interest in soil where nothing was sprouting, I knew this was a bad fit. Then I joined a book club. I stuck it out for three months, never finishing the books in time for the meetings. I'm not an intellectual, I'm not athletic, I'm not artistic—so what's left?"

For Robin and many others frustrated by trying to find positive ways to use their free time, a personal assessment of leisure needs may be helpful.

In a 1992 article in *McCall's,* Marlys Harris describes the development of such a leisure needs assessment by Steve Sumpter, a recreation counselor and director of rehabilitation services at a mental health facility in Dana Point, California. Sumpter suggests you begin by making a list of the five primary roles you play regularly and next to each list all the currently unfulfilled needs that, if satisfied, would make the role more satisfying, comfortable or effective. For instance, in your "parent" role, do you want to have more fun with your children? In your "self" role, would you like to be outdoors more?

Sumpter then suggests analyzing the list and choosing the five most important unfulfilled needs—even if they don't relate directly to leisure time usage. You can begin to see a direction for change if, for instance, you recognize that you want to think less and get your hands dirtier. Or that you long to learn more. Or that you want to try something you've never tried before.

Sumpter's assessment concludes with a plan of action. Next to each of the five most important needs, write down a way to meet each one. Whether you jot down signing up for a first aid class at the local Y or setting aside an hour on Sunday to read, you will find yourself beginning to develop a positive plan for enjoying your leisure time more.[5]

The possibility also exists that what you're really after is not an activity but a *lack* of activity—the chance to "waste" time. For some people, leisure time is best spent nondirected; contentment is found in tinkering, puttering, wandering or daydreaming.

"It took Kathy ten years to stop bugging me about finding a hobby," says Larry, the police officer we met in Chapter 5. "She's tried to get me to join a gym, collect coins, take up golf and set up a woodworking shop in the basement. She didn't understand that I wasn't looking for something to do. She loves to go out walking, and she takes cooking classes. I say that's great. But during my free time I'm happy to be left alone to do little odd jobs around the house or to wash and wax the cars."

Just how do we spend our free time? Over the years popular leisure time choices haven't changed. Americans spend their free hours most often in this order: watching TV, visiting people, talking, traveling, reading, participating in sports and outdoor activities, engaged in hobbies, taking courses in adult education and thinking or relaxing.[6]

According to a 1991 report in *The Futurist,* home-based activities will increase in importance through the 90s. During the 80s, while out-of-home entertainment grew only modestly (film box office revenues increased by 3 percent, attendance at professional sporting events by 5 percent and revenue for Broadway theaters was down by nearly 4 percent), in-home entertainment exploded. The annual growth rates ranged from 10 percent for cable TV subscriptions to more than 50 percent for video sales and rentals. Dictated by our hectic three-career lifestyle, convenience is a key factor in choosing how we spend our time.[7]

Leisure Time Abroad

Curious about how people in other countries relax and how much leisure time they have? Here's some international trivia:

- European countries with the most free time are Holland (49 hours each week), Switzerland (39) and France (32).
- In Japan, watching TV accounts for about half of people's leisure hours. TV is less popular in other countries like Norway, accounting for as little as 19 percent of spare time.
- Across the globe, six activities use up 80 percent of all free time—watching TV, getting together with friends, reading, playing sports and going to meetings and cultural activities.
- The Finnish and the Dutch take the prize as avid readers—an average of 5.5 hours a week per person in the Netherlands and 5 hours a week in Finland.[8]

Why do we choose what we do? "For me and Paula, it was a question of need, interest and priority," says June a 39-year-old banker. "Between work and our families, we rarely see each other, so we decided to spend Saturday morning together. We're best friends, but we're like day and night. She, being Mrs. Athlete, wanted to play tennis or go ice skating. I haven't been on skates since I was ten, and playing tennis with her would be a joke. I suggested taking a course at our Y. Holiday cooking? Pottery? Art appreciation? No good for her; she doesn't have the patience to sit still and concentrate. Finally we gave up and agreed to meet for breakfast and do what we both do well—chat."

A 1990 Leisure trends/Gallup survey of 5,000 Americans found that most Americans prefer to relax instead of achieve in their spare time. They gravitate toward familiar activities and those they learned when they were young. The interviewers found that the major motivators for leisure activities fall into nine categories:

1) Recuperative. Americans are basically homebodies who prefer sitting to standing, being entertained to entertaining and relaxing amid familiar and unchallenging surroundings. Ninety-four percent of those interviewed would choose to use their leisure time to recharge their psyches.

2) Tenacious. A strong tendency to finish what they start was reported by 95 percent of the people surveyed. This suggests that a person who makes a commitment to begin a new activity is likely to keep doing it. The key here is the promise of accomplishment.

3) Hands-on. We don't notice too many people outside cutting down trees and building homes from logs, but a lot still enjoy building decks, making their own home repairs and tinkering on their cars. Overall, 81 percent are motivated to work with their hands.

4) Sociable. Seventy-six percent of Americans say they are more sociable than unsociable. The younger we are, the more sociable we tend to be.

5) Intellectual. Given the time, 68 percent say they are intellectually curious. Activities that fall under intellectually

oriented leisure include reading, solving puzzles and taking courses.

6) Pleasure seeking. Overall, 64 percent see themselves as more pleasure seeking than not. They'd surely accept an invitation to spend a week on a tropical island, sipping pina coladas and soaking up rays.

7) Competitive. Leisure time competition is waning. For some Three-Career Couples activities like racquetball may yield to yoga.

8) Escapist. Reality is murderously difficult to escape. Among adults ages 30 to 34, only 50 percent tend to be escapists. Leisure is more than just a vehicle for escape.

9) Ambitious. Only 33 percent say they are ambitious in choosing leisure activities. It's about time we realize leisure time is not intended to win wars.[9]

In the long run, what you do in your leisure time is less important than how you feel about it. There is a link between your satisfaction with leisure activities and your satisfaction with life as a whole. Remember (we know, we know, we've said it before—but it's time again), there is no one master plan for everybody. Whether it's foreign coins, crossword puzzles, car racing or needlepoint, as long as it brings you satisfaction it's the right choice.

SPOIL ME, PAMPER ME, INDULGE ME...PLEASE?

If a little time-out for yourself is the ice cream cone, then a few hours of total self-indulgence is the hot fudge sundae. Hard to imagine giving yourself so much pleasure? Probably. But a half hour massage, a facial or a makeover at a nearby spa can be definitely worth the time and money. If guilt's a factor, make the treat a birthday ritual. If you can afford it, celebrate each month's anniversary of your birthday with some gift to yourself. Aside from the more obvious ways of spoiling yourself, how about—

- hiring an expert for a private lesson learning something you've always wanted to perfect. An ice skating lesson, perhaps? ballroom dancing? speed-reading? new ways to use your computer?

- fulfilling a long-term fantasy. Go up in a helicopter, ride in a hot-air balloon, parachute jump; try anything you've dreamed of but never dared to try.

- looking mystically into your future. Visit a psychic, get your palm or tarot cards read, have your handwriting analyzed. Do something totally spiritual.

- hiring someone to do the annoying tasks that drive you crazy. There are loads of competent people who'd love to pick up a few extra dollars by taking charge of your filing, bill paying, hard-to-make phone calls and mundane correspondence. You can pay someone to grocery shop, take your dog to the groomer, go to the post office for stamps, pick up your dry cleaning and wash your car and fill it with gas. Use that bonus time to soak in a bubble bath, play with your kids or catch up on your pile of last month's magazines.

- learning how to choose wardrobe colors that flatter you, accessorize appropriately and—for women—apply makeup to best accentuate your features. A consultation could change your total look.

- picking up a complete takeout dinner at a gourmet shop. Use your fine china, a linen tablecloth and nicest candles to create the perfect mood.

- playing hooky from work and sneaking off by yourself (or with a friend) to a matinee or a museum exhibit that's mobbed on weekends. Browse through every floor of your favorite department store, try on a dozen outfits you'd never dare to buy, linger with the newspaper over coffee and a sumptuous pastry. Be deliciously delinquent.

- hiding away in your own home all day and doing exactly what you want to! Sleep till 10; breakfast on chocolate cake in bed at 11; read old love letters; try on clothes from your college days forgotten in the back of your closet; eat peanut butter on white bread for lunch; reminisce through 20 years of old photo albums; play solitaire; play the piano; rent a movie that no one else wants to see; splurge on four slices of pizza for dinner; top it off with a Snickers bar nightcap. Calories? Fat grams? Worry about them tomorrow; don't spoil your perfect day!

SUMMING IT UP

In the fantasy world of the Three-Career Couple, there'd be 48 hours in a day, houses that would clean themselves with the snap of two fingers, built-in chauffeurs to drive the kids to afterschool activities and plenty of time left over for ourselves. But in the real world of the Three-Career Couple, our kids need us, our spouses need us, our bosses need us, our pets need us, even our dirty laundry needs us! We recognize that the absence of time for ourselves is a physical and emotional health hazard, and daily we face the challenge of trying to eke out any minutes for ourselves that we can find.

As a new Three-Career Couple, you'll find the real world a friendlier place if you incorporate the five "re's" into your daily life:

1) Revive yourself by carving out of your busy schedule some time for yourself—because you deserve it.

2) Renourish yourself with a daily dose of solitude—time to be creative or idle, to think or imagine or relax or dawdle or putter.

3) Rekindle the friendships that mean so much to you—with lunch, a phone call, a shared activity or even a written note. Good friends are hard to find, harder to keep and too important to be taken for granted.

4) Reenergize yourself with activities you enjoy. What you do is less important than how you feel about your choices. The name of the game is Satisfaction.

5) Rejuvenate yourself with an occasional pampering. Give yourself permission for a bit of self-spoiling now and then. After all, you are your most important asset; if you don't take special care of yourself, who will?

WE'RE IN CHARGE NOW

With that we've come to the end of the book, winding up not far from where we began. For only by restoring energy and balance into our three-career lives can we delight in the things that make the rest of life worthwhile: our loved ones, our home, our work. Only by taking good care of ourselves can we appreciate the true benefit of success—the luxury of time to do what we want to. And only by continuing our odyssey of redefinition, careful not to fall victim to trends and statistics, can we find happiness in the things that matter most in life.

Men must work hard to change the statistics that say even though they'd rather be good fathers than wealthy, way too few of them take advantage of their companies' paternity leaves. Women, becoming more practical and results oriented as they share more of the same career choices as their mates, must not be tempted to change positions with the men they've long sought to improve. Together, blessed with stronger marriages and more treasured children, we must prod each other to remember that our goals and aspirations can be more than dreams.

If we're going to be creative in the ways we devise to save time, then let's spend it getting to know ourselves better and become more accepting of our strengths and weaknesses. Only by making the reestablishment of our short- and long-term priorities of utmost importance can we deal with the stresses of time management, financial decisions, child care. Because we don't get to learn most of life's lessons until after we've lived through them, we're all finding our way together. And together we'll arrive.

CHAPTER ONE

1. The U.S. Department of Labor, Women's Bureau, "Facts on Working Women" (January 1992).

2. Susan Haywood, *Men Finally Beginning to Redefine Roles* (*Advertising Age,* November 18, 1991).

3. Elizabeth Wood and Floris Wood, *She Said, He Said* (Michigan: Visible Ink Press, 1992).

4. *Ibid.*

5. *Ibid.*

6. Ellen Galinsky, "Work and Family: 1992—Status Report and Outlook" (New York: Families and Work Institute, 1992).

7. Ellen Galinsky, Dana E. Friedman and Carol A. Hernandez, *The Corporate Reference Guide to Work-Family Programs* (New York: Families and Work Institute, 1991).

8. *Ibid.*

9. Frances Goldscheider and Linda Waite, *New Families, No Families? The Transformation of the American Home* (Berkeley: University of California Press, 1991).

10. *Ibid.*

11. Elizabeth Wood and Floris Wood, op. cit.

12. "Profile of Working Women" (*The Women's Record,* July 1992).

13. T. Berry Brazelton, M.D., *Working and Caring* (Reading, Massachusetts: Addison-Wesley Publishing Company, Inc., 1987).

14. The U.S. Merit Systems Protection Board, *Balancing Work Responsibilities and Family Needs—the Federal Civil Service*

Response (a report to the President and Congress of the United States, 1991).

15. Allison Clark Stewart, "Families Today" (*Good House-keeping,* February 1989).

16. Associated Press (*Newsday,* May 11, 1992).

17. Elizabeth Wood and Floris Wood, op. cit.

18. *Ibid.*

CHAPTER TWO

1. Sally Wendkos Olds, *The Working Parents' Survival Guide* (Rocklin, California: Prima Publishing and Communications, 1989).

2. Mary E. King and Janette M. Scandura, "Customized Stress Control: Identify Your Coping Style" (*Working Woman,* October 1990).

3. Cara S. Trager, "Counseling Plans Grow with Workplace Stresses" (*Crane's New York Business,* June 8, 1992).

4. Ellen Galinsky, Dana E. Friedman and Carol A. Hernandez, *The Corporate Reference Guide to Work-Family Programs* (New York: Families and Work Institute, 1991).

5. Herbert Benson, *The Relaxation Response* (New York: Morrow, 1975).

6. Kudos Pan Squares National Gallup Survey, January 1993.

7. *Ibid.*

CHAPTER THREE

1. Donald A. Tubesing, *Kicking Your Stress Habits—A Do-It-Yourself Guide for Coping with Stress* (Duluth, Minnesota: Whole Person Associates, 1981).

2. Gilbert L. Whiteman, Ph.D., *Management Skills Workshop—Managing Time and Stress* (Madison, Connecticut: Business and Legal Reports, Bureau of Law and Business, Inc., 1984).

3. Roy Alexander, *Commonsense Time Management* (American Management Association Worksmart Series, 1992).

4. Caryl Waller Kruger, *Working Parent—Happy Child* (Nashville, Tennessee: Abingdon Press, 1990).

5. Roy Alexander, op. cit.

CHAPTER FOUR

1. Elizabeth Wood and Floris Wood, *She Said, He Said* (Michigan: Visible Ink Press, 1992).

2. Arlie Hochschild, "The New Marriage Reality" (*Glamour,* July 1989).

3. Arlie Hochschild, *The Second Shift: Working Parents and the Revolution at Home* (New York: Viking Penguin, Inc., 1989).

4. Anna Quindlen, "Abhors a Vacuum" (*The New York Times,* September 10, 1992).

5. Frances K. Goldscheider and Linda J. Waite, *New Families, No Families? The Transformation of the American Home* (Berkeley, California: University of California Press, 1991).

6. Arlie Hochschild, *Second Shift,* op. cit.

7. Beth Sherman, "The Dirt on Men" (*Newsday,* September 26, 1992).

8. Jane Brody, "Rewards May Outweigh Stress" (*The New York Times,* December 7, 1992).

9. Dianne Burden, "Balancing Job and HomeLife Study: Managing Work and Family Stress in Corporations" (Boston University School of Social Work, 1987).

10. Sally Wendkos Olds, *The Working Parents' Survival Guide* (Rocklin, California: Prima Publishing and Communications, 1989).

11. *Ibid.*

12. Beth Sherman, op. cit.

CHAPTER FIVE

1. Ron Taffel, Ph.D., "The Real Trouble with Working Mothers" (*McCall's,* June 1992).

2. Findings of the National Commission on Children Survey of Children and Parents (*National Commission on Children,* Washington, 1992).

3. *Ibid.*

4. *Ibid.*

5. Elizabeth Wood and Floris Wood, *She Said, He Said* (Michigan: Visible Ink Press, 1992).

6. William Mattox, Jr., "America's Family Time Famine" (*Children Today,* November-December 1990).

7. Andrée Aelion Brooks, *Children of Fast-Track Parents* (New York: Viking Penguin, Inc., 1989).

8. Sally Wendkos Olds, *The Working Parents' Survival Guide* (Rocklin, California: Prima Publishing and Communications, 1989).

9. Ellen Galinsky and Dana E. Friedman, "Education Before School: Investing in Quality Child Care" (a report for the Committee of Economic Development, 1992).

10. *Ibid.*

11. Diane E. Papalia and Sally Wendkos Olds, *A Child's World—Infancy Through Adolescence* (New York: McGraw-Hill, Inc., 1993).

12. Deborah Bell, "Attention Working Women . . . Rate Your Stress Life" (*Redbook,* June 1990).

13. Sally Wendkos Olds, *The Working Parents' Survival Guide,* op. cit.

14. Elizabeth Wood and Floris Wood, op. cit.

15. James D. Eckler, *Step-by-Stepparenting* (White Hall, Virginia: Betterway Publications, Inc., 1988).

CHAPTER SIX

1. Ellen Galinsky and Dana E. Friedman, "Education Before

School: Investing in Quality Child Care" (a report for the Committee of Economic Development, 1992).

2. *Ibid.*

3. *Ibid.*

4. *Ibid.*

5. *Ibid.*

6. *Ibid.*

7. *Ibid.*

8. *Ibid.*

9. *Ibid.*

10. Karen Denton, Lois Theissen Love and Robert Slate, "Eldercare in the 90s" (*Families in Society*, June 1990).

11. Sharon Muir, "Women Taking Care" (*Network*, June 1992).

12. Beth Sherman, "When a Distant Parent Gets Sick" (*Newsday*, August 15, 1992).

13. Sharon Muir, op. cit.

14. *Ibid.*

CHAPTER SEVEN

1. C. Rubinstein, "Money Discontents" (*Psychology Today*, December 1981).

2. Sylvia Ann Hewlett, "Running Hard Just to Keep Up" (*Time*, fall 1990).

3. Deborah Belle, Ed.D., "Attention Working Women . . . Rate Your Stress Life" (*Redbook*, June 1990).

4. W. W. Meade, "Money Fights: A Report from the Marital Battlefield" (*Cosmopolitan*, August 1990).

5. Marjorie Hansen Shaevitz, *Making It Together as a 2-Career Couple* (Boston: Houghton Mifflin Co., 1980).

6. Hilton Times Values Survey, 1991.

7. "The Wage Gap—Women's Earnings and Men's Earnings," 1991 Fact Sheet (Washington, D.C.: Institute for Women's Policy Research).

8. Elizabeth Wood and Floris Wood, *She Said, He Said* (Michigan: Visible Ink Press, 1992).

9. *Ibid.*

10. *Ibid.*

11. Paul Strassels, "It's Your Money; A Spouse's Income Costs as Well as It Pays" (*Nation's Business,* March 1989).

12. Diane Harris, "Keeping More of Your Second Income" (*Working Woman,* January 1993).

13. Paul Strassels, op. cit.

14. Diane Harris, op. cit.

15. *Looking Ahead to Your Financial Future,* National Center for Women and Retirement, 1992.

16. *Ibid.*

17. Judith Beckman, "The 401(k)—Your Ticket to a Financially Healthy Retirement" (*The Women's Record,* February 1993).

18. National Center for Women and Retirement, op. cit.

19. Diane Harris, op. cit.

20. *Ibid.*

21. Jeanne Reid, "Married Couples Want It All: Two Careers Plus Children" (*Money,* March 1989).

22. William G. Kistner, CPA, "Tax Relief for Dual Career Parents" (*Healthcare Financial Management,* July 1992).

23. Jeanne Reid, op. cit.

24. Paul Sheldon, "Why Women Are Better Investors . . . Than Men" (a report for Prudential-Bache Securities, New York, 1992).

CHAPTER EIGHT

1. Elizabeth Wood and Floris Wood, *She Said, He Said* (Michigan: Visible Ink Press, 1992).

2. *Ibid.*

3. David Laskin, "Make Room for Daddy!" (*Redbook,* March 1990).

4. "Allowing Fast Trackers to Stay in One Place" (*Wall Street Journal,* January 7, 1992).

5. Elizabeth Wood and Floris Wood, op. cit.

6. Sue Shellenbarger, "Employers Help Men Adapt to Changing Roles" (*Wall Street Journal,* November 28, 1992).

7. H. J. Cummins, "'Family Friendly' List of Companies Is Short" (*New York Newsday,* November 15, 1991).

8. David Laskin, op. cit.

9. "Facts on Working Women" (U.S. Department of Labor, Women's Bureau, October 1990).

10. Jill Andresky Fraser, "Women Power and the New Age" (*Working Woman,* December 1992).

11. Felice N. Schwartz, *Breaking with Tradition* (New York: Warner Books, Inc., 1992).

12. "Facts on Working Women" (U.S. Department of Labor, Women's Bureau, January 1992).

13. Jill Smolowe, "When Jobs Clash" (*Time,* September 3, 1990).

14. *Ibid.*

15. Ellen Galinsky, Dana E. Friedman and Carol A. Hernandez, *The Corporate Reference Guide to Work-Family Programs* (New York: Families and Work Institute, 1991).

16. Elizabeth Wood and Floris Wood, op. cit.

17. Felice N. Schwartz, op. cit.

18. "Money and Making It" (a study conducted by the Roper Organization for Shearson Lehman Brothers, New York, 1992).

19. Fact Sheet, by the Olsten Corporation (Westbury, New York: 1991).

20. Julia Lawlor, "Companies Get a C for Sensitivity" (*U.S.A. Today,* November 15, 1991).

21. *Newsweek,* November 25, 1991.

22. Ellen Galinsky, "Labor Force Participation of Dual-Earner Couples and Single Parents" (New York: Families and Work Institute, 1991).

23. Alan Deutschman, "Pioneers of the New Balance" (*Fortune,* May 20, 1991).

24. Ellen Galinsky, Dana E. Friedman and Carol A. Hernandez, op. cit.

25. *Ibid.*

26. *Newsweek,* op. cit.

27. Ellen Galinsky, Dana E. Friedman and Carol A. Hernandez, op. cit.

28. Olsten Fact Sheet, op. cit.

29. Ellen Galinsky, Dana E. Friedman and Carol A. Hernandez, op. cit.

30. *Ibid.*

31. Sally Wendkos Olds, *The Working Parents' Survival Guide* (Rocklin, California: Prima Publishing and Communications, 1989).

32. Data from the U.S. Travel Data Center, 1990.

33. Marjorie Hansen Shaevitz, *Making It Together as a 2-Career Couple* (Boston: Houghton Mifflin Co., 1980).

34. Carol Lynn Mithers, "Whose Career?" (*Glamour,* June 1990).

35. Karen Levine, "When Spouses Compete" (*Parents,* March 1991).

CHAPTER NINE

1. Elizabeth Wood and Floris Wood, *She Said, He Said* (Michigan: Visible Ink Press, 1992).

2. *Ibid.*

3. "Index of Marital Success 1984–1988" (*Journal of Marriage and Family,* May 1991).

4. Michael Castleman, "Destress Your Love Life" (*Prevention,* June 1991).

5. William Masters and Shirley Johnson, *Human Sexuality* (Boston: Little, Brown and Company, 1985).

6. Elizabeth Wood and Floris Wood, op. cit.

7. Barbara J. Berg, *The Crisis of the Working Mother: Resolving the Conflict Between Family and Work* (New York: Summit Books, 1986).

8. "Long Distance Couples: No Extra Stress" (*Health,* September 1992).

CHAPTER TEN

1. Elizabeth Wood and Floris Wood, *She Said, He Said* (Michigan: Visible Ink Press, 1992).

2. "Media Myth" (*Working Woman,* February 1992).

3. Marlys Harris, "Five Words That Will Make You Happier" (*McCall's,* March 1992).

4. Brenda Ueland, *If You Want to Write* (St. Paul, Minnesota: Graywolf Press, 1987).

5. Marlys Harris, op. cit.

6. "Spare Time" (chart from American's Use of Time Project, University of Maryland, *American Demographics,* November 1990).

7. Al Lieberman, "Using Our Leisure Time" (*The Futurist,* September-October 1991).

8. Doris Walsh, "Foreign Leisure" (*American Demographics,* February 1987).

9. Jim Spring, "Nine Ways to Play—Reasons for Choosing Leisure Activities" (*American Demographics,* May 1992).